SILVER:
An Eclectic Anthology of
Poetry & Prose

SILVER

*An Eclectic Anthology of
Poetry & Prose*

EDITED BY

JOAN JOBE SMITH
MELANIE VILLINES

SILVER BIRCH PRESS
Los Angeles, California, USA

ISBN-13: 978-0615719832

ISBN-10: 061571983X

FIRST EDITION, NOVEMBER 2012

Email: silverbirchpress@yahoo.com
Web: silverbirchpress.com

Book Design: Silver Birch Press

Photo Credits: Scotto Bear, Emmanuel Boutet, Mark Christal, Des Colhoun, Mario Roberto Duran Ortiz, Eclipse, Aindrila Mukhopadhyay, Joan Jobe Smith.

The Silver Birch Press
SILVER ANTHOLOGY
is dedicated to
JACK MICHELINE
born Harold Martin Silver
(1929-1998)

INTRODUCTION

BY MELANIE VILLINES

If it weren't for the pervasive dust of Los Angeles—and my quixotic attempts to eliminate it, at least in my living space—the Silver Birch Press *Silver Anthology* might not exist.

One day last summer [2012], as I was in an alpha-wave-zen sweeping mode, an idea shot into my head—to put together an anthology of writing based around the theme "silver." I realized this *Silver Anthology* would accomplish a variety of objectives—celebrate Silver Birch Press, build a community of writers, find a memorable way to promote the imprint, reach out to writers who read our daily blog, create a sense of camaraderie and engagement, and just have some fun.

Rather than solicit submissions, I decided to make this an "invitation only" anthology—meaning I would have to invite the individual to participate or a colleague could nominate someone. For writers, I believe that prestige trumps just about everything—authors are always looking for ways to receive validation for their talents, and publication tops the list.

The day after my "sweeping" insight, I sent out emails to about twenty-five people asking how they felt about participating in an anthology with a unified theme—in this case, silver. Most responded and all except one person liked the silver theme. (And even that person came around and is featured in the anthology.) We also received some helpful advice—including a tip that we place a word limit on prose entries (thank you, Barbara Dahl).

Along the way, one writer nominated so many of her colleagues that I asked if she'd like to serve as *Silver Anthology* co-editor. I'm happy to report that this renowned and celebrated author—Joan Jobe Smith, founding editor of *PEARL* and *Bukowski Review*—agreed and has given her heart and soul to this collection. Joan has nominated fellow writers—and she appears to know everybody—has read every submission with care and attention, and has determined how the pieces flow in the collection. In all, the *Silver Anthology* includes the work of sixty-two authors—and Joan nominated more than half of them. Thank you, Joan! She even had the brilliant idea to feature a Beat poet with a silver connection (and allowed us to use her photographs of him).

Joan and I developed guidelines for the anthology, which I emailed to people who told me they'd like to participate as well as to writers that colleagues had nominated. The guidelines hit people's emailboxes around the middle of August 2012, citing an October 15, 2012 deadline for submissions.

In explaining the silver theme, the guidelines stated, "*The publisher is Silver Birch Press, so silver seems an obvious choice. But the selection really goes deeper than that. We like this theme because it's rich, varied, and offers a wide range of possibilities—from second-place finishes, to eating utensils, twenty-fifth wedding anniversaries, hair color, swirling fog, coins, bells, jewelry, the tin man, space suits, car bumpers, airplanes, family heirlooms and on and on. Let silver spark your imagination.*"

Along with Joan, I read all submissions and remain impressed with the quality and variety of the work—poems that are short, long, funny, sad, romantic, nostalgic, and much more; stories that are inspiring, absurd, scary, humorous, touching, and a great deal more; essays that are uplifting, enlightening, eye-opening, satiric, and lots more; novel excerpts and scenes from a play that leave us wanting more. And, in one way or another, all are silvery.

So here it is—from summer inception to autumn arrival—*Silver: An Eclectic Anthology of Poetry & Prose*. We hope you enjoy the collection. Thank you for reading it!

And P.S....living in L.A., I finally understand why my writing hero John Fante titled his classic novel *Ask the Dust*. The dust (much of it silver in color) does speak to us—as evidenced by the Silver Birch Press *Silver Anthology*.

PREFACE

BY JOAN JOBE SMITH

Silver, Silver Everywhere…

This bright collection of silver-themed eclectic writings and eclectic silver sightings in poems, stories, essays, screenplay, play, and novel excerpts is the first anthology I've ever co-edited, and thumbing through the pages and scrolling down the screen to read every silvery metaphorical word written by such a vast, vivacious, and diverse group of writers has been an inestimably amazing and blazing experience. Silver, silver everywhere and all those sparkling drops to think: Silver!

"Nothing rhymes with Silver," Beat poet, the legendary Jack Micheline told me in 1997 when I found out his real name was Silver. I strained my brain to dispute him, cleverly, but only thought of silly off-rhymes like pilsner, pilfer, willful, skillful—Wilbur? Oh, it can drive you crazy. They say nothing rhymes with "orange." But then, later, I thought: nothing rhymes with Micheline. Does it? Nothing rhymes with Smith, either. Oh, who cares? It was impossible to out-clever the foxy word-wise genius Jack Micheline—one of the most fascinating poets I've ever had the good luck to meet, and now the good luck to publish via this *Silver Anthology*. (Jack passed away just months after I had solicited his work to feature in my literary journal *PEARL*).

So, lucky me, I now thank Melanie Villines for thinking of this silver theme to launch her distinguished Silver Birch Press. An excellent idea and now the enlightening, entertaining finale of her great expectations fulfilled unfold for you in this silver book you hold in your hands. I hope you enjoy reading these fabulous luminescences as much as we enjoyed selecting them.

TABLE OF CONTENTS

SILVER BIRCH PRESS
SILVER ANTHOLOGY

WINSTON TONG

Shining, sterling, sublime,
Incandescent, incisive, immortal
Laborious, luminous, lambent,
Valued, venerable, versatile,
Elemental, enduring, esteemed,
Regal, reflective, radiant

Silver.

THOMAS KUDLA

SILVER BULLET

Time

is

our

silver

bullet.

CLINT MARGRAVE

THE NECKLACE

How little a thing is needed for us to be lost or to be saved!

—Guy de Maupassant

I found your necklace
this morning.
It was there, by the bed.
Its silver fishing wire chain
tracing spheres in the carpet.

Maupassant wrote a cruelly ironic
story once about a necklace,
that turns out to be a fake,
sentencing a young woman
and her husband
to ten years of poverty.

So now, as this ornament
hangs over my hand,
I cannot help
but remember this story,
and how simple the object is
that breeds such a ruinous fate.

WALTER DE LA MARE

SILVER

Slowly, silently, now the moon
Walks the night in her silver shoon;
This way, and that, she peers, and sees
Silver fruit upon silver trees;
One by one the casements catch
Her beams beneath the silvery thatch;
Couched in his kennel, like a log,
With paws of silver sleeps the dog;
From their shadowy cote the white breasts peep
Of doves in a silver-feathered sleep;
A harvest mouse goes scampering by,
With silver claws and a silver eye;
And moveless fish in the water gleam,
By silver reeds in a silver stream.

BILLY COOK

SILVERWARE
intimacy comes and goes
like flashes.
silverware;
always with us no matter
what cities we're living in
restaurants, diners, cafes
strange houses
where I've taken strange meals.
the fork I'm eating pasta with
never changes
and the spoon I stir my
coffee with could be the same...
so, after all,
you are here.

intimacy comes and goes
lightly, like flashes.
tableware cleared away
replaced with clean
new forks and knives,
where, even though your sleeve
is not brushing mine,
even though I can't quite
sense the damp smell of you
after a morning shower,
eating eggs and buttering toast,
a fork is still a fork
a knife still there to remind
me that what has been cut
can be cut
and cut
again in as many different
➤

shapes as I can imagine—
and, after all,
you are here;
in the metallic click
against my teeth
bitter and
sweet
through cold and
heat
in a meal I once cooked for you.

BARBARA ALFARO

IN THE POEM

for Victor on our Silver Anniversary

I remember you in your red robe,
standing in a triangle of sunlight
as you feed our cats, put coffee on,
and break bread into pieces
for the birds outside in the snow.
You give me a poem you have written.
In the poem, what is best in me is
exaggerated the way truths are in dreams
and reading it, I see I am loved.

TIM WELLS

TALVISOTA

Silver hairs are still distant but worry you, though
every one of mine is testament to time well spent.
Attend to the dancefloor, the heart's
sweet business; now is the hour for
midnight meetings, whispers and murmurs.

You stir the coffee in my cup, proffer sugar
knowing I will refuse but accept yours,
low laughter as you lose plays at love.
A corner turned without coaxing,
off comes a ring pulled from a faintly resisting finger.

(based on Horace's ode 1.9)

MORIAH LACHAPELL

SILVER BELT
I dreamed
a woman
placed
a belt
of silver
around
my waist.

She was
pale
brunette
small
intensely
beautiful.

I woke
wondering
and the
answer
came
it is
passion.
➤

The
ardor
of
what
it means
to be
woman
wife
mother
lover.

All
contained
by a
silver belt
around
my
waist.

DONNA HILBERT

ICE
Friday night,
the middle of December, Dad
comes home drunk dragging
a tree.
He starts with the lights,
untangle, test.
He starts with me,
wants to know
why I'm clumsy, slow.
I try not to listen
as I bend
hair pins into hooks
to hang the colored bulbs,
until one shatters in my hand.
Clumsy! Stupid!
Words circulate like wind
I barely feel.
I drape the scarf
of icicles
over my arm,
separate, then hang
each shining sliver
until the tree and I both
shiver:
twin conicals of ice.

DONNA HILBERT

SWEAT
Consider sweat,
lowly wet product
of glands:

the salt mines
the stoop labor
the proletariat

of the body
at work in the matrix
of skin,

moistening each union
that arches or bends,
folds or grows hair

or extends
to touch the body
of the other

to touch the skin
of this world:

the sole of the foot,
the lips,
the palm of the hand.

DONNA HILBERT

WHERE IT HAPPENED

At the seam of water and sand
a lone blue heron stands.
And in the placid sea
its distant kin: the pelican.
On such mornings
all birds are silver, all words are song:
silver water, silver light
birds in flight
and after.

Weeks ago, sirens
lured me from my work
and on my perch
above the beach, I watched
as lifeguards pulled
a girl from water to sand.
There is no way to sing this.

It is noon:
the light is not silver,
nothing is placid
the spectral birds elsewhere,
but two policemen are here
with a man and woman. The parents.
This is where it happened.

I didn't see her face
that day, only her torso
her pale arms, still legs.
And her swimsuit,
her scarlet swimsuit.

DIRK VELVET

LA VOIE MARITIME DU SAINT-LAURENT
i should not
have gone in
that far with him

the waters were too harsh
the waves black
beneath
the silver

the bottom
current
pulled me in
and
my son out

for one
forever moment
i lost touch with him

the waters had him
more
than
i did

i did not
see his body
under the water
when i
took him back
➤

it was all luck
or
a
god
that gave him back to me

when we go back
to the water's edge

i kiss his forehead

and thank
the
mishigami
for not taking
my
son
with her

(Lake Michigan, Wisconsin, USA)

BARBARA EKNOIAN

ICE SKATING AT HUDSON COUNTY PARK

I see the lake outlined
with Christmas lights.
from the top of the hill.
The white ice looks like
a round birthday cake,
the piles of snow
scalloped
along the edges,
whipped frosting.
We hurry to put on
our silver blades
in the rental shack.
An iron stove stands
in the center
keeping us toasty
until we skate outside
in low thirty-degrees.
My feet are numb;
I think it's frostbite.
We head back up
the hill for home
while tears freeze
on my cheeks.
I can't feel my toes.
Then suddenly Danny
appears out of darkness
and tags alongside us.
My face flushes.
I feel warm again.
Danny is walking us home
and, just maybe,
he likes me.

BARBARA EKNOIAN

EARLY OCTOBER

I sit in a windowless office,
with gray walls in the Accounts
Payable Department.
I hate paying my own bills,
never mind tending
to an endless stream of invoices.
I can't wait for my vacation.
It's early October and we set out
for our trip from New Jersey
through Connecticut, then Vermont
on our way to Montreal.
It's the height of the fall season.
Trees crowned with orange, gold,
and rusty brown leaves
border the highway.
Vermont is a picture postcard:
cows and horses grazing,
church steeples sprout up on hilltops,
no factories in sight.
Pastures quilted in green and bronze.
I forget my dead-end job,
as we travel
up and down the hillsides.
The car seems to rise and fall
with the silvery sound of Pavarotti
singing on the radio.
I'm in the final scene of a great movie.
The colors surround us gloriously;
the road ahead is golden.

SANDYLEE MACCOBY

SILVER SKATES

Kate, The Ice Goddess, was a champion figure skater during World War II and a star attraction when she performed for the soldiers on the little circle of ice set up in the ballroom of the Copley Plaza Hotel. Only sixteen years old, she was beautiful and exciting to watch, like her idol, Sonja Henie. She closely resembled Sonja with her pert, pretty face and her silvery blond hair worn in the pageboy style of the 1940s with silver netting to keep it in place. No more than five feet tall, with shapely legs and small, pointed breasts that were visible under her sequined jacket, she smiled a dazzling, toothy smile that drew warm and friendly laughter from the sad and weary soldiers. When she twirled, the spotlight lit up her shiny silver panties with lace fringes beneath her sequined costume bringing roars of appreciation from the crowd. She made simple jumps on this round sliver of ice, but stopped and started so that her silver blades twinkled in the light. Performing for the soldiers was something Kate liked to do. Their love for her touched her heart. Performing for the soldiers was a lot more fun than competing for a national title.

It wasn't that The Ice Goddess minded competing, since she always won. She knew the judges liked her best of all because they thought her so pretty, and her mother kept them happy by inviting them over for drinks on a regular basis. Since the age of five, her whole life had been skating. She had attended professional school, which tailored the academics to her practice schedule. She had no close friends, and she sometimes wished she were like other skaters who went to a regular school and had sleepovers. Naturally, since they weren't stars, they could melt into a crowd, something she could never do. Wherever she went, she was recognized and asked to sign autographs, whether she wanted to or not. But she had learned that being a star meant it was her duty to please the public.

Photos of herself on the ice at competitions and exhibitions were a regular feature on the sports pages of *The Daily Record* and her mother kept several albums filled with those newspaper clippings on the table in the living room.

Kate's mother's major worry now was a little girl named Sondra, age nine, who was also invited to entertain the soldiers because they whooped it up so much when she skated. The little girl's father, a rich lawyer, had recently hired Mr. Johnson to watch over her because there were strangers and competitors out there who did not wish her well. She had recently received anonymous letters that frightened her, but with the arrival of Mr. Johnson she felt secure and well protected and her family no longer worried about her safety. He seemed to appear out of nowhere and dutifully carried her skates along with a black leather case containing a duplicate of her skating music (records in those days). Making this duplicate skating music available was his idea because he suspected her exhibition recording might get badly scratched or cracked by people working behind the scenes who wanted her to fail. At the skating club's Christmas pageant where she was featured along with The Ice Goddess, her record was found to have deep scratches and Mr. Johnson was able to replace it with the duplicate recording.

Sometimes Kate heard people whispering that Sondra would someday become famous like her but she paid no attention. After all, Sondra was just a little girl and wasn't beautiful and sweet sixteen like herself. How could she consider the child a threat? But the skating world of coaches and parents was beginning to take notice of this little girl who could jump higher and spin faster than The Ice Goddess, and skate with absolute abandon on that tiny bit of ice at the Copley Plaza Hotel. The little girl's nickname was The Red Flash and she liked to wear dark red velvet costumes with bright red sequins that lit up like tiny, dancing flames when the spotlight touched down on her.

Kate was awed by the presence of Sondra's powerful bodyguard, Mr. Johnson, who sat close to the ice and watched his charge with a special intensity. Large and friendly, with a dignified demeanor, he dressed immaculately in a dark suit and tie and often gave her a kindly smile. One day when she sat near him, she observed that his feet were very big and that his shoes were newly shined.

Never without his silver-rimmed glasses, Mr. Johnson usually sat alone, and when Kate, The Ice Goddess, took to the ice, he sometimes dozed off until awakened by applause at the end of her program. He never went to sleep when The Red Flash was on the ice and usually disappeared when the little girl skated off to the standing ovation of the soldiers. Observers nearby said that he seemed to vanish into thin air. There one minute and gone the next. A few minutes later, he could be seen waiting patiently outside the dressing room where Sondra removed her skates and put on her warm woolen coat. Rumors circulated that he might have magical powers.

Recently, Sondra, The Red Flash, had been getting more fans than Kate, The Ice Goddess. Was it because she was a little child and the audience was awed by her athletic and artistic gifts at such a young age? Kate's mother was worried.

"Not good, not good," she muttered with fierce intensity to her daughter. "Smile more, Kate. Maybe that'll do it. Tomorrow night is the last performance."

"But, Mummy, I smile all the time! I know the soldiers love me. I can see it in their faces!"

"Sure, sure. But face it, girl, The Red Flash is getting standing ovations! I've already spoken to the lighting people to work the spotlights on you more. You need to dazzle! You're The Ice Goddess, after all! They have to love you best!" Her mother paused, then added in a low voice, "We must stop her."

"Who?"

"We have to stop The Red Flash. Do something!"

"Like what?" Kate was bewildered. What could she do?

"You could hide her skates."

"But there's that strange man who's always with her! He carries her skates and her music!" Kate cried.

"When she's in the dressing room, he's not there."

"No, that's right. She's alone."

"So?"

"So what am I supposed to do? I don't want to hide her skates! Anyway, she might find out."

"Look, I have an idea. You're always first to appear because you're the star...so maybe when you finish your program you could drop some dimes around on the ice. Nobody would notice and if they did, they'd think the money fell out of the pocket of your silver jacket."

"Then she'd slip on the coins, Mummy."

"That's what I'm thinking."

"She'd fall and could really hurt herself."

"That's what we want, isn't it? Then she'd be out of the picture."

"It's wrong, Mummy. It's a bad thing to do. That poor girl!"

"Look, your stardom is threatened by this little girl and you don't even realize it!"

"How can she be a threat, Mummy? She's only nine years old!"

"When Shirley Temple starred in a movie, all the adult actors on the set were very nervous."

"Why?"

"Because that cute little girl stole all the scenes! That's why!"

"Well, skating for the soldiers isn't like being in a movie and besides, they love me."

"Not as much as you think. So that's why we have to do something. Besides, Sondra doesn't need to be a star like you do. She'll have so much family money someday she won't know what to do with it!"

"I'm sick of being a star, Mummy. Can't I be like other people?"

"No. Your father ran out on us, remember? So you don't have a rich daddy like Sondra. I have to put food on the table every single day, and I scrimp and save so you can be a star. Right now we're in line to get advertising contracts, maybe even a screen test so you can follow in Sonja Henie's steps. Skate for the movies and make millions like her!"

"So I should drop dimes around on the ice after my program?"

"Absolutely."

"Even if I don't want to?"

"Yes! For me, Kate."

"I'd do anything for you, Mummy."

"Good, so it's settled. Tomorrow night, the last night of the show, okay?"

"Okay."

The next night, Kate, The Ice Goddess, skated perfectly. During her final spin, she threw ten dollars worth of dimes across the ice, but nobody except Mr. Johnson noticed what was happening. Sondra would be skating next so he closed his eyes and dreamed of a young woman with silver blond hair who was tossing silver dimes up into the air from a high balcony. Watching them fall down to the frozen ground, he turned them into snowflakes that soon covered the courtyard below. On awakening, he stared at the coins that had been scattered across the ice and within minutes, the coins melted into clumps of snow.

When Sondra, The Red Flash, appeared, she was smiling with joy and jumping higher and spinning faster than ever because snow was swirling all around her and the spotlight was picking up the sparkle of the silver snowflakes falling on her red velvet dress.

PAMELA MILLER WOOD

SILVER PAIL

The housework whore comes to my door,
    carrying her silver pail

She scrubs my brown wall, with a sponge and Pine-Sol,
    while I drink my golden ale

She dusts my shed, and makes my bed,
    and cooks for me with honey

What could she want, with this dirty haunt?
    She never asks for money

Some may think her problem is drink,
    but I state she's just nice

Others say, there will come a day,
    when I will pay the price.

(From *Charles Bukowski's Scarlet* by Pamela Miller Wood)

Beat poet Jack Micheline (1929-1998) was born in New York City as Harold Martin Silver. He is pictured above at the Jack Kerouac Conference in Boulder, Colorado, during the 1980s. (Photo: Mark Christal)

LINDA KING

JACK MICHELINE

Jack was a poet
  always on the move
  reading
  reciting
  painting
   fluid Jack
    fluid in New York
     fluid in San Francisco
     fluid on the streets
      head hanging
       to the side
        something wonderful
       something guilty
      something stupid
      something profound
     something wild
  winner of the big six
  with 1-2-3-4-5-6
I sculptured his head
  in one day
   morning to night
    Jack painted pictures
     during breaks
      and signed them
       with a flourish
        Jack Micheline

He knew he was great
painting from the tube
smearing the paint
with a few rags
divinely recording
no cruelty in his heart
no vengeance in his verse
no self pity
always out there
loving the sun
the silvery moon
the birds
the sky
the poor
the ugly
the fat
the misfits
the gays
the hurt women

that was Jack Micheline
tasting
writing
teaching us all
something about being free
something about clowning
If you heard Jack Micheline read
you'll never never forget
the rhythms of Jack Micheline

Jack made you

want to sing

Jack Micheline

Mich-O-line, gas-O-line

Jack-O-Jack-O Jack-O-line

Jack is back

Jack has pack

Jack in act

Wacky Jack

Jack the Crack

Jack needs a pack

Jack is back

Jack in sack

no tack Jack

Jack makes tracks

Fact

Rack

Smack

Attack

Poetry stack

Jack-O

Jack-O Jack-O-line

Mich-O-line, Gas-O-line

Mich-O Jack-O Mich-O-line

JACK MICHELINE

FRED VOSS

THE SILVER MAN EXPRESS:
A LITERARY PROFILE OF JACK MICHELINE
—after reading *Night City Poems* (1996)

I am standing at my lathe carving out a train wheel for Jack Micheline.

Jack Micheline was one of the best of the Beat poets. Changing his birth name of Silver for Micheline, the tire brand, Jack was a true child of the streets and roads of America in the tradition of Walt Whitman's "Song of the Open Road" and Jack Kerouac's *On the Road*. His poems were written on trains and buses and rooftops and in diners and bakeries and racetracks all across America in places like San Francisco and Berkeley and Chicago and Los Angeles and Brooklyn and Harlem and Greenwich Village and he was a true Beat poet because he loved and was one with the common man and the downtrodden man as all truly spiritual men are. When he mentions a city or a bus stop or a racetrack you know he's been there, gotten the dirt and the smell under his fingernails, rubbed shoulders with the people. Like Buddha and Whitman and Wordsworth walking on their feet and Kerouac riding in his car, Micheline is always moving ahead in a loving, inspired embrace of the universe ready to give his energy and sympathy to any who might need it.

He was a poet of anger, anger at the dark side of America, where worship of money, success, and power can become a form of fascism. He wrote fierce beautiful elegies for Harlem prostitutes and poor lonely artists and poets and musicians and carpenters and waitresses and poker players and dreamers who became victims of drink or drugs or mental hospitals in our cold, lonely cities.

He was a poet of humor and childlike wonder who wrote of the joy of Bernie walking five miles to eat good hot chicken soup and kreplach and cream strawberries in some Greenwich Village diner

(Night City Poems[1]) or the hats, lipstick, and garters of his Russian Jewish Aunt Tilly with her five dead husbands and her bagels and hot water bottles, or being in bed with red-haired Erika as he thinks of steak and onions and love money madness in America *(Wormwood Review: 37)*.

His poems were often half chants, and he often read them accompanied by a jazz saxophonist like Zoot Sims or a bassist like Charles Mingus. His poems were improvisational and earthy and uniquely American, like the best of jazz. During a great Charlie Parker solo in Kerouac's *On the Road,* bebop listeners in midnight nightclubs were inspired to yell out "GO!"—and that was Micheline, always going and going, like those Micheline tires, like the trains that Whitman and Kerouac loved, like the cars that Kerouac and Cassady drove all over America in joyous driven search for IT.

Zen monk. Romantic poet like Wordsworth writing his lyrical ballads for the poor folk of rural England. Holy saint and fool like Prince Myshkin in Dostoyevsky's *The Idiot,* whom everyone calls an idiot for his naïve simplicity but loves for his Christlike, childlike sympathy and wisdom. Angry friend and protector of the poor and victimized. Wild celebrant of mountains and flowers and women's legs, tireless wanderer of this land Woody Guthrie said belongs to all of us. He was all of these.

And I step up to my lathe and turn a dial and guide a razor-sharp cutting tool into the train wheel I have clamped into the chuck of my lathe this day in my imagination, and carve the wheel down for the train Whitman and Kerouac and Cassady and Micheline rode. It is a train to freedom, to beauty and a heart-stopping Louis Armstrong trumpet solo echoing down a New Orleans alley, a train to justice and the joy that made us jump up and down when we were three and the wildflower on the hill and it leads us to Jack Micheline waiting for us at the end of the line to put his arm around us and read us his poems that will make us glad to be alive.

---

[1] *Night City Poems,* 1996, handmade photocopies, spiral-bound, purchased by Fred Voss from Jack Micheline for fifty dollars.

Fred Voss (left) and Jack Micheline during Micheline's last reading on June 9, 1997 at Vinegar Hill Bookstore, San Pedro, California. (Photo: Joan Jobe Smith)

FRED VOSS

HOW IT GOES ON

This morning at 5 a.m. as I wake up to sit
over this white sheet of paper a little bit
of Jack Micheline is alive in me.
I think a little bit of him jumped into my soul
when he looked out of the side of his eye
at me before he got up to read
with the jazz saxophone in the bookstore
shortly before he died.
A little bit of a silver star
above a rooftop
in New York and maybe
a little bit of Jack Kerouac too.
Just the tiniest little bit of a spark
and the hope
that that spark will someday light the world on fire.
Just a little bit of Jack Micheline
a little bit of his childlike eye
and a grin
he wore maybe because he somehow knew he would live
in me.
Just a little bit of a silver star
from the earliest days of the universe
and a smile
full of truth stronger than steel
and a Mingus bass riff so alive with the soul of Man
on the streets of the city
and a hope that good men everywhere will have justice
at last
and that there is something that was not made for death
and Jack Kerouac
and maybe Jesus Christ and Buddha too
in me
and now
in you.

JACK MICHELINE

A CHILD WALKS IN A DREAM

A child walks in a dream
Her eyes dance in the night of stars
Someday when the moon is full
The gypsies come home
They will come home forever
And all the boats that never sailed will sail forever
And all the flowers that have not grown will bloom forever
A child walks in a dream
And all the stars that have not shone will shine forever
And all the children that could not dance will dance forever
A child walks in a dream

JACK MICHELINE

EVERYWHERE I GO

Everywhere I go is beauty
trees illuminated
street lights glowing in the darkness
I want to run up to strangers and kiss them
but there is too much noise
men kill each other
I'm sick and tired of seeing sad faces
stop that bastard machine
everyone is God and Holy
a spike is ripping my throat
I smell a fragrance of a rose
everywhere I go is beauty.

Jack Micheline (right) accompanied on saxophone by J.J. during Micheline's last reading at Vinegar Hill Bookstore, San Pedro, California, on June 9, 1997. (Photo: Joan Jobe Smith)

JACK MICHELINE

BLUES POEM

I got no smile cause I'm down
I carry a horn to blow in all these streets
A solo riff out of my head
How could you ever know I feel
So high on life and feet and ass and legs and thighs
That I can rise and dance with all the stars
And I can eat the moon and laugh and I can cry
The dark caves of cities hungry streets
The tired faces dark and dreary bent
and all the death it dies
I let it die
I lift my horn and blow some sounds
Some sound for kids to come
Some unborn sun
in darker streets than mine
Magicians carry wings so they can fly
Let's blow a horn and love
Let's get on it and ride
and laugh and dance and jive
Let's shake the dead and let the downers die
The magic of the singers warms the earth
A song
A poem
Some paradise of mind
I got to smile now
I'm feeling good
The city street
The palace of my mind

FRED VOSS

ART THAT ROARS

Machinists tape paintings of their old classic cars to their toolboxes
and stare at them

like they were Picassos

lines

of chrome side strips and bumpers and white roofs and green
hoods thrill

their hearts as they stand before them with fingers to chins

and deep thoughtful expressions on their faces

they drive

those old cars to work and gather round them in the gravel parking
lot at lunch

and let themselves feel the aesthetic pleasure

of how far apart and shiny their dual exhaust pipes are

how soft

and well-stitched their red tuck and roll upholstery is

authentic

orange California license plates from the 1950s are Cezanne

peaches

thick

un-dented chrome bumpers gleaming in the hot L.A. noon sun van
Gogh

sunflowers

as they walk around those cars and peer in their windows and ooh
and aah

like those art lovers

they'd always made fun of in High School

➤

4-on-the-floor gearshifts

and tachometers and speedometers that go to 130 mph

in Mustangs and T-Birds where beautiful women cross their legs

beside them is their idea of a Mona Lisa

worth ogling

they can stop

slapping and punching and poking each other and fall in love

with these cars

they have restored with a touch as delicate

as Michelangelo's

cars that can roar

and shoot gravel and speed out of that parking lot after the quit-work whistle blows

      deadly

as rattlesnakes

and as the steel mill smokestack belches red-hot stinking orange sparks

the machinists step up to those cars and stroke them

unashamed

to fall in love with art that can go from 0 to 60 mph

in 7 seconds.

FRED VOSS

HOW MANY TIMES CAN WE FOLLOW
DANTE DOWN INTO HELL?

I still have moments when I look around and wonder what I'm doing
in this machine shop
with these men
wearing steel-toed shoes
acting like I never read Shakespeare
Dostoyevsky Plato
I will never tape a poem to the side of my toolbox like
a drill chart
or a picture of a 1932 Ford
or a woman in a skimpy bathing suit

all

these poems forming inside my head secret behind my sparkling
eyes
as my machine plunges smoking drills through slabs of steel
am I insane
between tin walls where never once in 100 years has a poem
been mentioned
where men would rather go to County Jail
than read a book of Keats
looking
for poems in tool steel worm gears
bloody knuckles
eyes
of old men who can still break out dancing

like 5-year-old boys

because they've made a tool bit shave through aluminum until it
shines
like silver
there are enough poems about sunsets
about leaves

falling onto grass

how many times can we follow Dante down into Hell

admire

the ceiling of the Sistine Chapel

pretend

each drop of sweat that ever rolled down the skin of these men
gripping

      machine handles isn't

a poem

each nut and bolt

tick of time clock

ache of bone

sacred

each hand

dripping with machine grease and cutting oil the one

that made

the world?

STEVE WILLIAMS

STEEL STORY

My first framing job in 1992 was building four-story hillside houses in Brisbane overlooking Candlestick Park. The boss was using a four-wheel Gradall with a hydraulic boom to lift a thirty-foot I-beam above the frame to lower it down a pocket in the middle of the frame and set it as a center post. The boom was fully extended, dangling the steel like a needle on a thread when it started to tip and begin its slow motion tumble down the hill. Steel and tractor headed a hundred feet downhill. Everybody scrambled. I was three feet away uphill. The fat kid carpenter working down below ran faster than anybody ever seen and just got away. Nobody hurt.

Last week, almost twenty years to the day, we were lifting a twenty-two-foot, 8x8 inch I-beam into a pocket I cut into the floor joists above (our ceiling) to replace a bearing wall between the kitchen and living room. There will be continuous steel posts at each end of the beams from the third to the sixth (top) floor. A hoist is put on the roof centered on the beams and a cable is dropped through a hole down to each unit to lift the beam starting with the third then up to the sixth. My unit is the fifth floor. The beam is lifted with a fabric strap hooked to the cable.

Thursday, I got there and the steel guys had lifted the beam about eight feet up, and then my job is to be ready to make any fine-tune cuts to make sure the beam has a unobstructed path up to the floor above. It was clear above (I did a good job!) but the steel guy wanted me to enlarge the floor opening at one end to make it easier to weld the steel post to the beam below that had been installed a day earlier. I blew up at him, offended because the day before he'd looked at the opening and said it was okay.

"Now you want me to get under a hanging load (1500 lbs $\pm$) to cut out a few more inches?"

I refused to do it. A twenty-four-year-old, Julian, grabbed my saw and did it. He's one of the bosses, actually. There were a couple of other bosses there who had no comment to my refusal. It seems nobody talks back to a big guy barking.

Fifteen minutes later, the beam was being hoisted the last couple of feet into the opening. There was a steel worker at each end twisting and guiding the monster and I stood two feet off to the side watching. Pop, Pop, POP, **POP, POPPP** the strap strained and broke and the beam fell to the concrete floor as fast as an apple. The building shook and shouts came from all over the jobsite. Nobody was hurt.

I saw Julian the next morning and asked him how well he slept. He said he couldn't. He didn't tell his family it was so frightening. They had been working under beams like this for two months. I told the top boss to have temporary posts ready to support the load before anybody goes under. It takes five minutes and thirty dollars worth of lumber to make it safe. He agreed.

MARK WEBER

I USED TO BUILD HOUSES

I used to build houses, but
my heart was mostly in jazz
then
when I added a few years to my life
I grew to love building houses

...silver on the shores of far away

further along, I am less concerned
with absolutes—it is not uncommon to
hear my mouth say that I
don't know

so much is in flux...

(or seemingly in a flux) (I don't know for sure)

"...the shores of silver far away" is a line of J.R.R. Tolkien's
becomes the dream nowadays

JOE HAKIM

heartbeats and headaches

These mornings are like a smack in the gob.
The white-wine flavor sunshine
pours over my tongue, into my mind.

It's hiding in plain sight, tired and cracked,
a raw nerve exposed to cool air.
Tobacco and dust, the smell of lemon
sheets and the sleeping stack of socks

are embroidered into the walls, as the clam-
shape clock ticks languidly. Thoughts of
ships anchored in mud rush through me.

In these minutes when we awake
and the silver sky is caught on the washing-
line, nothing else matters aside
from our heartbeats and headaches.

(from *No Light/Might Escape,* 2011)

ADELE STRIPE

MERSEY HAIKU

1.
watching the gauche bridesmaids
stumble
i eat ice cream
and stare at the sun

2.
chasing his footsteps
through bright bluebell woods
eyes sore from easter pollen

3.
cheap wine sours on my tongue
it helps me do nothing
just like li po

4.
tracing the silver birds' path
beneath oriel windows
he kisses my neck

ADELE STRIPE

MYTHOLMROYD HAIKU

1.
this is my cradle;
asleep in your warm chest hair
your heartbeat a lullaby

2.
the sun hides behind
st. john in the wilderness
our lips taste the hot raindrops

3.
the fading confetti sticks
to the wet stone walls
like fallen apple blossom

4.
palms sticky from pine resin
the transparent moon
sucks the light from my fingers

5.
cycling in the morning sun
the sweet smell of popping plants
hangs in the june air

ADELE STRIPE

QUIETISM

I listen to you
tap tap tap
on an underweight keyboard

gain some kind of comfort
from the rhythm
and your cough.

Outside the snow is falling
like moths burned by
a nitrate moon

and silence envelops
these once busy streets,
footsteps are cushioned
in the ginnel of dust
where the pink reflected halogen glow
is the tone of my cheeks
just half an hour ago.

Mogwai's
"You Don't Know Jesus"
plays a codeine drone
from the speakers downstairs
somnolence drifting up through the air,
condensation in fuzz guitar notes.

I open the window,
hang my legs off the sill,
let the snowflakes collect
on my Clara Bow lips; soft and sweet
I dream of vanilla

and listen to you
tap tap tap
on an underweight keyboard
on this February night
under stoned
Titian clouds.

TAMARA MADISON

SHEDDING

If I watch
I can see myself
shedding the leaves
of the day
onto my unclean
kitchen floor.
If I'm not careful,
if I turn on the radio
for example
the sound of the voices
will cover me
like an oily skin,
heavy, weighted.

So I put myself
on a ship.
It's a wooden ship
with a warm shape.
The current is smooth.
The images of the day
tumble behind
in my wake.
The moon rises
and washes them
clean and they shine
like chips
of blue silver.

TAMARA MADISON

RIVER

In dreams my roads fill
with clear sweet water
flowing gently; there is nothing
to carry, I can swim
beyond the flooded buildings,
through countryside covered
with this vast river
to anywhere I need to go
where warm cool water lifts,
surrounds me; it is silver,
it is gray, it has no color, it shines
like fish, is dark and soft
like sleep. When I wake
the bell pricks like pins
and I want that water
to fill my veins and carry me
on that river back to sleep.

Tamara Madison

YOGA TEACHER

She told us she was very old named a number
in the sixties, older even than our parents.
She wore a black unitard that displayed
an elastic body at least as nubile as our own.
Her hair spouted from her crown in a silvery
blond ponytail and her face was smooth
and shiny. With her amazing body she revealed
the wonders of yoga; we eagerly copied
the poses—downward dog, salute to the sun,
cat, moon, lion. We marveled as she performed
isolations, making her internal organs hop
side to side like a twitchy garden hose.
She would ask Kregg, the only boy among us,
to demonstrate a pose with her. She found him
as fascinating as we did. One day she told us
about *auras*, and offered to tell us what color
ours were. Kregg's was white—deep and spiritual.
Lissa's was red for passion, Kathi's blue for thought.
Mine—she didn't want to say. Sometimes,
she said, you meet a person with a black aura.
Stay away. I never went back to yoga class
after that, but I'm doing yoga still,
with silvery hair and an aura as shiny-black as hers.

ZACK HUNTER

BROKEN SOUL IMPROV

I

I was sitting full-lotus around a fire that was whispering symbols in a tipi in the desert listening to the wind howl when I closed my eyes and left. There is a latch that clings to our souls that I know how to undo with a bit of focus. The method is there waiting to be learned intuitively. Passing through the loudest possible explosions of atomic blasts from within, I ride an eternal detachment through an organic tube twisting out of control.

Then it all falls into place with a fold and comes back one piece at a time, almost looking like a cartoon but obviously much more sophisticated. I am in the body of a person walking through a forest in the dead of night. The moon through the dancing silhouette of the canopy is somewhere in between the color of bone and chelated metal and duplicates a shining. Three echoes sag beneath it elliptically rainbow—like mirrored teardrops or breasts. The atmospheric friction eats a meteorite with a fiery streak.

My new eyes move back down now to the darkness that surrounds me. Everything everywhere glows gold with a palpable symbolic indication that is flowing omni-directionally from and through. Sung by the insects in an echo-location sequence. I wouldn't be able to see these hands without eyes so wide you could stick your tongue in and bend the lens. There's a light-blue neuro-electricity coming out of my skin and touching the surrounding electromagnetic layers and rippling off into the sea of air.

Above me, there is an owl watching. It hoots, and I can see the patterns illuminate and scatter off of any reflective material in these woods. Absorbed by the decay. In the flash of that moment, I could feel in my hands what it was saying to me. I could see it seeing me, saying hello to the vagabond, or transient, currently occupying this sector of the abyss.

Walking further now along a game trail through the ruffling of fallen leaves and low level plants. It can be seen both by the moonlight and the reflection of the bug songs reacting with the electric night. I don't know where I am going, not that it matters. What seems random in the moment may reveal the secrets of time in a resonant memory uploaded to a genetic server rolling its eyes at matter.

An intense and nauseating sickness is rising inside of me as I attempt to gracefully make my way through the not-so dark. The serotonin in my stomach screams, "INCOMING!" Overtaking every sense, every intuition, and every thought—I keel over to the side of the trail and explode a torrent of projectile vomit that from the sound alone I can tell launched over a few feet away and came out fluidly, instantly, and powerfully, carrying out and away everything I ever was on every layer. Feeling reborn a thousand times and gagging with a choke.

The hum and vibration of a swarm of a million bees escaping their hyper-spatial hive overtakes me, and I glow crystalline moments of partitioned awareness that branch off into the eyes of consciousness. My heart is juiced and bioluminescent honey spews from my core. Lying down in a patch of clover looking up through the tears, wiping my mouth with my sweatshirt sleeve, hundreds of ladybugs crawl onto me, and I don't even notice them—I am orbiting a star and twitching with a moan.

This mouth, acidic and bitter, reminds me of how I got here, who I am, and what I am doing.

II

I get up into the flowing golden symbol darkness, again feeling lighter than a red helium balloon and rising. The ladybugs all take flight right on cue. There's almost a magnetic pull guiding me to follow in this direction. I am now passing through an open meadow on the peak of a mountain. I can see at least thirty miles in both directions. To the valley and to the sea. All the sleeping people—their dreams are dancing a perfect synchronization spiraling outward and down.

Stopping to press my palms together with eyes closed to glow a lunar mudra, a bobcat a bit larger than a full-grown German Shepherd emerges from the grass and sits down next to me gazing out. Looking like an Egyptian depiction, it purrs a low frequency for me. I can feel it soothing the wormhole reaction inside my solar plexus spinning. It licks its lips as I pet its head looking into its eyes, and we both disappear back to wherever it is we were going before crossing paths and forming a dimensional knot in the night.

I can see, hear, and feel everything that ever was and ever will be. Even the nothingness in between. Automatic and alive, we are the technology of light. Paradoxes spur like the so-called impossible corners of a sphere. This illusion is as brilliant just as much as it is fucked beyond reasonable repair. Going in both directions. Human concepts made up and applied. Made to think we're confined to a small strip of human perception. I never expected my detachments to understand. Or anyone.

Further along the trail, I find myself at the edge of a cliff. My old leather boots kick dust and small rocks off of the edge and, even in the stillness of the night, I hear nothing down there. Nothing but wind. The moon shines a synthesized sound like the motion of the dispersion of dust and keeps rhythm with a percussive tap of bones or glass vials clinking in stretched-out slow motion.

Somewhere, sometime, I am back in that tipi around the fire listening and watching Marco sing our way through the ceremony. It's like some kind of distant memory now. That was the waypoint that led me here to this body. To this cliff. To this moment. Under an almost-full moon swirling around in the soup of the stars blinking their reminders. I can't believe how in just a hundred or two hundred twists and turns this planet makes how strange things could get. Blown out of proportion and insane. Corrupted by a greedy concept. Destroy to recreate. I get lost imagining the billions of years of weird that has had an opportunity to expand the recrystallized gimmick of the observed universe.

III

No. This isn't real. I have surfed and bailed on these waves long enough to know better now. I've had enough. For years. This whole situation I can smell reeking from its current and future cancerous demise leaking into me. My little capillary. The tumors are sprouting on the dandelions of the nervous souls glowing. It takes meditation to figure out how to cut the cords to the leech that feeds on the blood of a soul-sucking boredom. The lack of ideas is the fuel that it feasts to expand. It projects an invisible electric fence of fear in the form of numbered documents and deadlines. I can't even laugh at it anymore. Not even up here and this high.

And so this is where I wind up. Out in the desolation of a perfectly symbiotic piece of, well, *mostly* undisturbed land in resonant bodies all reacting to the same intuitive desire. Here I am tonight. Feeling the atmosphere chill goosebumps down to my withered bones. It gets colder in the stillness. I rock back and forth involuntarily from the pressure of my beating heart pushing on the inner vasoconstricted walls of whoever it is that this is.

I take a deep breath and stand up feeling phantom wings sprout the feather weightlessness lifting my rise. There is some kind of tree growing out of the side of this cliff. I am not sure what kind it is, but judging by the way it is thriving particularly so well in this spot, I am guessing it must love the big air pockets the roots get from the continual erosion. It grows up and out over the tremendous fall that nothing without wings could survive.

Something about it is calling to me. I can't remember the last time I even climbed a tree, which is something I used to love to do more than anything. Just being up there, above everything. I feel the cold bark dig into the spirals of my hands and fingerprints as I put my weight and faith onto the tree and make my way up, putting one foot on one slippery branch at a time. There are spiders that have probably lived their whole lives up here wondering what it is that I am doing. I cast a peaceful, nonthreatening vibe apologetically to my proximity.

Slowly, with Ganesha grace, I make my way to the farthest branch that reaches as far as it can out and above the cliff. I let go of my last support branch that I was holding onto for security. It is just me and my balance keeping me on this tree. I inch myself closer as the branch begins to bend. This is the very farthest anyone could ever possibly go and live to tell about it. Only a bird or a centipede could make it any closer. I am watching the tiptops of trees for miles swirl around in a rainbow dance of accelerated consciousness. There is a pattern in the way they move, and I decode and follow it to stay perfectly balanced. I raise my arms up from my sides with the phantom wings. A galactic wind blows through my invisible feathers giving way for lift, but I remain.

All of the golden symbols that had invaded my altered perception in the night flip like a switch in that instant. Void of color but shining a liquid quicksilver now. There's my reflection in the mirror of consciousness itself that drips its gravitational pull trickling into all. This human body begins to melt. Dripping droplets of quicksilver from disfigured boots not clinging to the branch. I am every drop falling down now through the darkness. Feeling every one that splits and merges. The body has completely dissolved into the metallic silver energetic serum slipping away. Getting caught in the high winds. Hundreds, now thousands of observation points scattered and raining down gaining speed in a crescendo of butterflies and death. In each silver drop is the fast-forward reminder that all of this has already happened. The roar of wind shaping every single one of me. Looking out in all directions, about to splash on the jagged cliffs below—

I open my eyes and gaze into the Celtic knots forming in the fire in the tipi. Marco is dolphin-headed on the other side singing ultrasonic cymatics silently. Underneath the surface of the soft statue of windows that I am is an automatic process that collects.

"What is fluid cannot break," he was saying to me in the mind.

GAIA HOLMES

FISH

"There are plenty more
fish in the sea,"
he tells you with conviction
knowing, as he does,
the whole spectrum
of glitter, silver fin and gill.

He knows fish
that would shock
with their electric,
sheepish fish that graze
on plankton, sea furze
and the moss
that clads shipwrecks.

He knows fish
that you can trust
for their regularity,
fish that get high
on the lights
of midnight trawlers,
fish that freeze
mesmerized
by the clank and hum
of ocean liners.

He knows fish
that fall in love
with pebbles,
fish that get giddy
when wind
fingers the waves.

He knows fish
that would gracefully
take your hook
into their mouths
without wincing.

BREEDING

The clocks are breeding.
Their birthing ticks
rock the house.
Their wind-milling hands
un-latch a breeze
weighted with chime
and cuckoo call.

Time judders and skits
across the carpet
like silverfish,
its intricate minutes
flashing in the sunlight,
patterning the walls
with chips of light.

Things are moving fast.
Face numbers are a blur
of tocking sums.

We had grown
slack and soft
from all the waiting
but now time
is taking over the house.
It has climbed into the kettle
and boiling will not kill it.
It has moled its way
into the bread and bled
into the water
and we too are full of it,
unable to remember
the slow texture
of hours unfolding
and the way they used to
spiral down our fingers
curl up
and doze on our laps.

GAIA HOLMES

FEBRUARY

Things tell lies
in the treacled-light
of my carnival lamp.
The ashtray appears
to be full of diamonds.
Outside frozen toads glitter
like bashed-up emeralds
on the lid of the pond
and you leave a trail
of spider's silver
across the map
as you weave yourself
away from me.

Jeri Thompson

SILVER
I give myself like a coin,
Silver for your pocket.
Brilliant when minted,
Tarnish has worn at my edges.

As of late, your tarnish;
Clandestine calls lost in lies,
Messages unanswered,
Abrupt schedule changes.

Time has come to shine,
Polish my crevices.
I will learn someday
Why the gift I gave you
Was not
Silver.

ANDREW HILBERT

A TALL CAN, PLEASE

he's worked hard for
these quarters and dimes
yet the corner store guy
still rolls his eyes
when the change falls on the counter
to be counted.

CHIWAN CHOI

dimes

summer had just started
and i didn't have a job
like many of the other kids in my 11th grade class did.
i'd get up and look for reasons to get out of the house.

i didn't have a car yet either.
my blue bomber, the 76 monte carlo that would
eventually catch fire and blow up
on gramercy drive, wouldn't be until my senior year.

one morning,
i was up early enough to see my father leaving for work
dressed in his paint-caked work outfit,
a bucket of rollers and painting spatulas
in one hand, pulling on a spray machine with the other.

we caught each other by the door.
he looked at me as i rubbed my belly
under my t-shirt.

i smiled,
trying not to really think about what he did
with his days,
the work he'd committed to for his family
remembering the day, the only day
he ever took me to work with him.
i'd tried to help that day
the way i'd seen sons do in movies
handing him the tools he needed
as he repainted a tiny 1 bdr apartment
in koreatown by himself
for a 100 bucks.

➤

son, he'd said as we sat and ate the lunch mom packed us,

i never want you to do this kind of work.

he put his bucket down and opened the door
and as my mom moved toward him with his bento box,
he pointed at me without looking
told her to make sure i stayed home all day.

don't let this boy out of the house, he said.
she nodded.

hours after he was gone,
she did let me go.
i took the bus to the westside
to meet up with the fellas
for football at stoner park
and we ran like the boys we weren't able to be
in our other countries—
korea
phillipines
china
japan.

and we ran for the summer
that had just begun
until there was a collision,
mack's newly braced teeth slicing through
the skin of my forehead,
filling my eyes with blood
and the world became a beautiful red.

at ucla emergency room,
i begged the nurse to not call my father
and they stitched me without notifying him

➤

but when i got home that night,
my father was sitting on the couch in the living room,
his jaw tense,
mother silent next to him with her hands on her knees,
and when he saw the bandage on my head,
he screamed at her,
telling her that this is what happens when we don't listen
and he sent me to my room
from where i could still hear him scream.

i got into bed and stared at the ceiling
and he came in
and he sat down on the bed
and i looked at him, blurry through my tears,
and he smiled again
and he asked me if it hurt
and he handed me a small jar.
i found it today, he said.

it was a jar of dimes
but they looked different,
less shiny.

silver dimes, he said.
maybe it will be worth something one day.

he got up to leave.

dad, i said.
i don't know what i'm supposed to do.

he turned around and walked out
without a word,
leaving me in that room

➢

where i'd one day steal my brother's old typewriter,
leaving me
to search for the rest of my life
for the value
of what he'd found
of what he'd given me
of that thing he'd hoped
so much
would save me.

MEGHAN PINSON

TODAY YOU OPEN THE WOODEN CABINET

Today you open the wooden cabinet
I call my heart and paint it red, the red
of cherry-blossom, of almost lucky,
of tongues and embarrassment.
Ten thousand pages it took
to shrug off the loose garment of marriage,
the damp gown of motherhood,
this silver ring

Then you turned your head
and ten thousand kisses flew
straight into the sun.

BEN MYERS

YOUR BREATH COMES ACROSS THE PILLOW LIKE A SAVANNAH BREEZE

Your breath comes across
the pillow like a savannah breeze.

Your mouth has produced
no tumbleweeds

while you
were sleeping.

The coyotes have been
cast from the chrome kingdom

and outside the first drops of
rain fall like a

drunk violinist on the steps of
the marble cenotaph.

BEN MYERS

AND NOW THE INTERNET IS HAUNTED BY DIGITAL GHOSTS

And now
the internet
is haunted by digital ghosts.

Sometimes
in the middle of the night
you can hear their
tiny tinny voices
screaming down
the wires.

I want to
cut
those cables
and set them free

and make them
real.

BEN MYERS

SHOPPING LIST RAIN

I went for a long walk in the metallic rain and
the noise it made was like a shopping list

"stamps wax pomegranate"
it whispered into my ear.

ANN MENEBROKER

PHOTO COMPOSITION

it's the way his hips poke out, one foot
resting a little to the side, holding more of
his weight than the other, his large right hand
holding onto a hat, wearing an ill-fitting suit
which looks sexy on him, dressing
him for this wedding day, and she, beside
him, in a satiny silver dress, slim, beautiful
and probably smelling of wonderful perfume, that
makes me feel their love and need of each
other, the direct "here we are" into the camera
and then eighty-one years of age later, older than
history and opportunity, separated by
ill health and finally, by death, he fumbles
and trips over life and falls into that mystery
orchestrated by an unknown song
where she has gone.

(Originally published in the chapbook
The Measure of Small Gratitudes, Kamini Press, Sweden 2011)

DIANE EAGLE KATAOKA

TRAJECTORY

Friday night begins with
promise, suspending
stars just beyond reach,
snow couched high
around the pool like
sleeping mastodons.

He soaks in the Jacuzzi,
steam an aura around him.
I, dolphin swimming
without arms,
breach and dive
in the deep end.
Warm water dizzies
my skin, piquant shiver
of cold air above.

Wrapped in silvered cloud,
we laze across weekend sky
in short delirious naps,
making love in the snow
while iced breezes
riffle our skin.

As summer rises off
crust of winter, slow
action of chemicals
reveals clear print of
me as the other woman.

He might just as well
have slapped me across
the face for the sting
of the pain.

LUSH LIGHT

Autumn sun
eager to meet
its daily quota
rushes into
canyons and valleys
with silver-edged
copper light
burying day in
rose-fired rays
swooning into
soft fog of dusk
leaving it to the moon
to bring mountains
back into relief.

EXHALING WINTER

Snow retreats up mountain walls
pulled on a timed tether

Grasses and brush spring back
to vertical
avalanching winter's skin

Along a rivulet, pale shoots test the air
while catkins of aspens
shiver in silver light

I smell spring long before color
flushes tree and ground

Tentative breaths still redolent
with winter's waning chill
ride over my skin

Whispering a promise of warmth
Inhale gently
gaining green. (—All poems from the chapbook *Snow Globe*)

GERALD LOCKLIN

HORACE SILVER: *SONG FOR MY FATHER*
    (*In Memoriam:* Leonard Feather, Jazz Essayist Extraordinaire)
Horace's memories of childhood
Are of a musical family
That congregated at musical parties.
His father was Portuguese,
Raised in the Cape Verde Islands, but having come
To America at an early age.
He was a strong, gentle man, with a sense of humor,
And a love of living and of life.
He was simply a good father to a good son.
In the cover photo, John Tavares Silver
Sports a cigar, straw hat, and open smile.

I always wanted to give this CD to my children,
Not just because it is one of the jazz classics,
Instantly recognizable as such,
But so it would be for them
Not a call for veneration of myself,
But as a testament to my love of my own father,
A decent, intelligent working man, and veteran of WWII,
Spent in the boiler room of a destroyer escort
In the South Pacific, who returned home,
His health broken, and died at 50
Of a diabetes-related heart attack, a week before
My graduation from high school, but not before
He had indelibly modeled for me (though, in my case,
Only to be grown into after many years of immaturity):
What it means to be a man.

The saxophone solo by Joe Henderson
Remains, (alongside Joe Gonsalves' legendary
"Crescendo and Decrescendo in Blue,"
From *Ellington at Newport*)
One of the two final assertions
Of what manhood once stood for:

➤

Passion, Procreation, Protecting and Providing for,
And, if necessary, dying for one's family.
Thus, the F-minor bossa nova blues
Moves from mellow confidence
To the rhythmic/melodic apotheosis
Of piano, trumpet, sax, bass, drums,
Horace, Carnell, Joe, Teddy, Roger,
Swing, Bop, Reflection,
A nautical knot of the chordal, elegiac,
Quintet-essential Harmony,
The present ongoing beyond analysis,
The paradigm of memory and desire
Pentagrammatic denouement from tension,
Shakespearian in aspiration,
The "Shock of the New"
(Thank you, Robert Hughes)
That we inhabit only in The Jazz Moment.

It was the thesis/antithesis of the male and female
Bodies and souls into the dream
Of a newly powerful, compassionate America,
Which has only now begun
To come into existence.

GERALD LOCKLIN

PIECES OF SILVER: **"SEÑOR BLUES"**
   (Liner Notes: Leonard Feather)
Horace always had "Cool Eyes" for his band.
Here he features Donald Byrd on trumpet,
Hank Mobley—tenor sax.
Doug Watkins—bass, and an 18-year-old
Louis Hayes on drums
Horace and Hank were among the many protégés
Of Art Blakey as Jazz Messengers.
The other three hailed from the hotbed of Detroit.
Their leader, spared by his upbringing
From the cloud of alcohol and drugs,
Led by example and intelligence, often deferring
To his supporting cast. He could delineate
A quiet ballad, and change his paces with
A pregnant pause, as in "Shirl," melodic
Inspiration from a lady friend. The ballad form
Brings out the best, the romance, in the breast
Of the male beast. In "Camouflage" and
"Enchantment," the pianistic virtuosity emerges.
Rhythmic innovations allow for power of thought,
The minimalistic silences that were saturating
Abstract expressionism, Theatre of the Absurd,
The neo-classicism of John Cage,
Reversals of sonic metaphors,
Tropic spice and cold pellucid clarity,
Doubling of the sax and trumpet
In New Orleans contrapuntal,
In competition and coordination,
The ringing single notes of linearity
For which he'd become famous,
A-typical octaves, cerebral contrarieties,
As mallets dictate percussion discipline,
Confusing only to the dilettante,
                              ➤

But "Señor Blues" is what we came to hear:
The minor-key in triple meters,

Six or twelve beats/counter-beats.
As with Beethoven's Fifth,
As with Ahmad Jamal's "Poinciana,"
There are no boring or inferior
Patches/passages/pastiches
Lurking in this masterpiece.
Mister Horace Silver has taken the reins, firmly,
Charged and changed aesthetically,
Irrevocably, unforgettably, as when
The Master Poet, Ron Koertge and I
Played and replayed "Señor Blues"
Over Budweiser at Mary Garfono's
Pizza joint on Valley Boulevard,
Alhambra, California, at the bottom
Of the hill of L.A. State, 1964-1965,
The year my students taught me how to
Dance freestyle and march freestyle
To Pershing Square for Civil Rights,
And, after the conflagration of Watts,
Mourn the end of the era in which
Good will could still trump race and class.

That was almost fifty years ago, but still
The strophes and antistrophes, calls and/
Responses of "Señor Blues" ring true,
An anthem of the dream that hid itself
In the unconscious of America, still today
In struggle to expand beyond the
Confines of the Jazz Continuum, the refuge
Of the reconciliation figured forth in
Surges/hesitations, contemplations and
Crescendos, aspirations and ascendancies
To the soul/rebirth, spiritual re-embodiment of
Señor Blues in all his splendid shining Forth.

GERALD LOCKLIN

STREAKS OF SILVER: **NNENNA FREELON**

I fell in love with her years ago
At the Jazz Bakery in Culver City
When she was re-emerging
After a hiatus devoted to her family.
Sure, there were a few streaks of silver,
But they only highlighted her beauty,
Not to mention the experience and maturity
She now added to her extraordinary talent
And the youthful spirit and playfulness
That she has never lost, will never lose.
It was her rendition of Stevie Wonder's
"My Cherie Amour" that I took with me
From the club that night, and sang in my head
For weeks thereafter, finally trying and failing
To add my pitiful emulation
To my "poetry" reading repertoire.
That holiday season I sent everyone copies of
Her album tribute to Billie Holiday.

Now, in 2012, at the Orange County
Performing Arts Center, I gaze at and listen to her
From the nearest seats of the horseshoe mezzanine.

She offers "I Feel Pretty," and she should,
Because she is. "The Very Thought of You" captures
The loneliness of road trips away from loved ones
At the center of one's life. (She adds a bit of scat,
But hers is tasteful, discreet, and original.)
"Got to Get Off This Merry-Go-Round"
Stirs memories of when a bunch of us beer drinkers
In the 49ers Tavern would rise in a unison whiffenpoof
Medley of lamentations, except that hers are always
Excursions into a parallel universe of rhythmic
And harmonic improvisations, ours just travesties.
Charlie Chaplin's "Smile" remains tangentially faithful

➤

To his triumphant return to the Academy Awards,
But builds to a vocal power in its final notes.
"You and the Night and the Music"
Bears witness to her generous deferrals
Of the spotlight to her accompanists.
She honors the lyrics of Cole Porter's
"Get Out of Town" and the "Skylark"
Of Hoagie Carmichael and Johnny Mercer,
But displays her wit and contemporaneity
In her own composition, "Cell Phone Blues."
Intelligence illumines every melody she voices.
On the *Homefree* CD, her son Pierce Freelon
Will add Rap vocals and MC musicianship
To the Traditional "Lift Every Voice and Sing,"
And it is no surprise that the resident vocalist
Of the Kennedy Center would close with
"America the Beautiful."

But it's on her versions of
"If I Only Had a Brain,"
"I Say a Little Prayer,"
"The Tears of a Clown,"
And "Nature Boy"
That I become aware of what intrigues me most:
The ways she frames, mimes, dances, personalizes
Each song with her fingers, hands, arms, and postures,
The slight and subtle transformation of Music
Into Gesture, Nuance, Theater, Ballet.
No one does it better; Sinatra would applaud.

Nnenna, we will never meet, but I will take
The absolute perfection of your performances
Into eternity with me. A loving admirer: G.L.

GILLIAN EATON

SWIMMING AT 50 DEGREES

I head down into the blue,
light glinting up from the silver floor,
in latex cap, ill-fitting goggles,
black swimsuit, old body—
fat round the middle like an arctic seal—
and each degree slaps me hard.

> *Some swimmers strip down*
> *in the blanched air like Latvians*
> *or Finns who can skim*
> *down the Baltic's stone gray waves*
> *with no lust for Fiji or the Balearics.*

> *Young men, sleek and swift, enter*
> *effortlessly, others bunch and brace*
> *elbows up, slow to submerge;*
> *some, lean and wrinkled Prufrocks,*
> *measure out their days in laps.*

Moving fast through the water
toes and fingers stiffening
in short-lived weightlessness
eyes adjusting to the white space,
I let in patches of cold,
soft knives of ice,

shadows of the sharp wave,
as in ritual preparation
as in perfect practice
for the last plunge, the final floe,
the sheet that'll ship me out
when the end is near enough,

➤

so that when it does come,
as it must, it might appear
familiar and timely,
like a returning wanderer
or a welcome tradition
in a sane and loving land;

but now, spread for a moment
under that bleak blue sky
on winter's meniscus
the carrion crows and gulls
circling low and loud,
not yet, I think, not yet.

JAX NTP

MEDUSA SONATA

Dreams are the aquarium of night—Victor Hugo

We argued over the process of marinating
tofu — you left me at the   A q u a D o m   — staring at the
giant kelp
                    swaying behind thick glass

          like naughty skirts, mute sirens seducing
my defenses. The rapture of her lyrics
          encircle
my limbs, exposing
          tendrils of vulnerability.

On the scale of   d e s i r e,   you weigh more than
          the immortal medusa because you are blessed
                    with the gift of death. Sometimes suffering
can be beautiful, but it will never be black
          and white like the cross-sections of a dragon fruit.
          My body is a broken
                    metronome, a rusty
                              mondayblue masonjar,

a translucent sea wasp chiffon. I   f i s h   for a heart that
glows
          like moonstones and the power to recite the mariner's
                    song, "fair wind and following seas." A farewell or a
curse?

I   w a n t   to swim in your waters — merge with bright min-
nows,
          plankton, and pirate ships. You've left me suffocating
                    with tunes like gold ribbons of honey dipped and
swirled

          ➤

94

in strong black tea. I   y e a r n   to be someone who needs nothing,
something that needs
          n
            o
              t
             h
               i
              n
                g, but even moon jellies rely on the mercy
        of ocean currents
                to propel them forth
                        towards their d e s t i n a t i o n.

Jax NTP

plucking out the sutures

i'm not the bride
of death, but the   bed
where she lies.

       she does not   speak   to me,
            nor i to her.
       when the moon is bald and horny
i look   at her face   and wonder what
       she is remembering
in   our   silence.

my father balancing
me on my bike,
my first false memory of
            falling.
the way watercolor
       drips
     off the page.

no more breastplates
and shin-guards,
what a naked arena.

words akimbo to my intentions.
such haphazard seams.

c l o s e n e s s   has nothing to do with distance.
pure iron comfort.

not maternal   nor erotic
but a   nostalgia
     for both.
the location   where i want
my   ashes   scattered,

     my last thought
     before sleep.

Jax NTP

not mandatory, compulsory

the medulla oblongata supplies impulses
to kill caterpillars then complain
that there are no butterflies,

this is what happens when we forget.
teach me how to carve anatomical figures
into daily things: the shapes of bones into coat hangers,

the texture of cartilage into tempered glass coasters,
teach me how to reveal numismatic qualities of aged coins
from the exquisite sea corpse holstered in a blue venetian bottle,

how to remove the green plant that lives between our mandibular
central incisors, how lanolin delays decay. the minutia value
of nerve signals between the interlude of night and day

not melting, rotting.

JENA ARDELL

SILVER: 4 CONNOTATIONS

SILVER IN SAN FERNANDO VALLEY
(FAST, SHINY AND NEW)
Two beams
silver headlights
slice through the night sky,
               like bullets,
 down Mulholland Drive

Lights divide
cutting quadrants
across bedroom walls
before disappearing
into the darkness
  quickly
      fleeting,
         now
      careening,
    down
       Topanga
       Cyn.
     Blvd.
where partygoers stay awake
'til the stars are swallowed
by the San Fernando Valley fog

that pesters L.A. drivers
 Freeway road rage
  as sunglasses
    slide
       across
polished dashboards

tall
    wide

SUVs & Hummers
each, only holding
        one person

This morning
make-up smears
above
    &
     below
glassy pupils,
  metallic shadow to the brow
(what
    was I thinking?)

I walk to the mailbox
in pajamas,
    bed-head reflection
        in shiny numbers

No one will see
me
      because no one
    does the speed limit

It finally came today
    The steak knife
that cuts through a shoe sole
  (or at least that's what
the infomercials say)

I don't care if it can't
    I just wanted something new
          ➤

SILVER
(OLD AND USED)
Wooden coffee table
slick with dew
A rare roadside treasure
free to those who can haul it away

Two giant
wet glasses stains
in the center
accented by
silver spills
of God-knows-what

The voice inside my head
says,
  "Take me,
    make me new."

SILVER ON THE 101 (CLOUDY, UNCLEAR)
Slinking down the 101
    Abrupt stops.
Cherry taillights
  explode color
    into monotone sky

squinting to see
    through silver fog
an infinite amount of steam
    sl ug gish ly   sails
into my car
    through open windows
          ➤

constant streams
        of streetlights
slur into the air
        as we
(this fog, these strangers, myself)

        sit in the San Fernando Valley
sedated.
        wondering what minuscule detail
will distinguish this day
                        from the last

SILVER (STALE, SLOW)
Stale
silver
smoke rings
moseying carbon monoxide

stiff
disguised cylinder
nicotine
&
tar
traces of ammonium
& cyanide

smoke me.

JOHN BRANTINGHAM

HOW I FELT

There was one time in the dead
center of summer after we'd
had a Santa Ana, and the glass
on the windows seemed ready
to melt but the Santa Ana was over
and storm clouds had moved in. A snap
of lightning and all the rain in the world
landed on our street. It poured for three
minutes and moved on. When it was gone,
the street steamed and hissed
until it was dry again. Last night,
I woke up at two in the morning.
You were lying perfectly still,
and you didn't know I was watching you.
When I saw you lying there so quietly last night,
that's just exactly how I felt.

(from *East of Los Angeles,* Anaphora Literary Press, 2011)

JOHN BRANTINGHAM

YOUR FAVORITE JAZZ RADIO STATION

Even way out where no one lives,
you can hear talk radio—mostly
people saying the same things
your least-favorite uncle tells
you after a couple of drinks.

Closer to the perimeter,
country music, news radio
and oldies stations help to keep
you awake. You dream about sitting
in the back seat, listening

to your parents arguments,
and driving to Mt. Rushmore.
Then come classic rock, alternative
rock, and classical music
at about the same place

in the suburbs with fights
in minivans between the generations.
But when you get far enough
in the city that corruption
and brutality is painted

on the walls near the freeway,
you can always find a jazz station,
not at the physical center,
but somewhere a little to the left,
where the real city moved

➤

when the downtown apartment
buildings were torn down
and replaced with warehouses,
museums, bus depots, train stations,
silver giant office buildings

that you're not supposed to go into,
parking garages, and overpasses.
It moved with the people
who scrub the office buildings
and spend long days in little booths

just inside the parking structures.
They work the warehouses
and guard the museums.
The existentialists in town
were born there or moved there

for a couple of years after college.
Most of the people who can hear
your favorite jazz radio station,
don't listen to it. The existentialists
have too much revolution to think about,

the kid who works the parking booth
listens to the Morning Zoo on K-Something,
and the people who are allowed
into the office building dream
of news reports from Wall Street.

Only four people you know actually listen
to jazz radio, and you know for a fact that
each one of them, without exception,
gets up every morning and says,
"God, I love this city."

JOAN JOBE SMITH

BY THE LIGHT OF A SILVERY WATTS RIOTS MOON

A go-go girl in the raw, out of the frying pan and getting used to dancing in the fire at The Fort, that stinky hellhole beer bar, August 12, 1965, unaware that the Los Angeles Watts Riots had exploded in the night as I lay sleeping, not knowing that it was an Apocalypse Now, not subscribing to a newspaper, my three kids not home watching TV, away on a camping trip in Big Sur with my girlfriend Madge and her kids, I went to The Fort as usual to work the night shift as a go-go girl. So I had no idea why the freeway was barren of rush hour traffic jam at five p.m., only my blue VW Bug putt-putting along, did not know why the gravel-greasy parking lot at The Fort was not jam-packed with workingmen's pickup trucks, motorcycles, and beat-up used cars, completely empty except for my boss Mick Jakson's silver gray Porsche Spyder.

The Fort's door—though usually wide open that time of day, Happy Hour, till eight p.m. when the blues or rock band came on and prices doubled—was closed, but only half-locked, I saw, when I jiggled the handle, heard loud jukebox music inside. Yanking the doorknob, kicking the door, I finally got it to open, sunset light pouring into the place and turning the black empty space to sparkling orange glitz. Without the sweaty, drunken men reeking inside the dank and dark, I could smell how awful The Fort, a beer bar, stunk all by itself of mildew, dry rot, urine, beer mold, decomposing murdered corpses maybe—and a Hound of the Baskervilles-sized Norwegian wharf rat in its pear tree.

The Fort had been built to look like one. Had to be to protect its particular iniquitous den and din fortressed and self-contained to ward off the onslaught inclemencies of its Fate of Geography. Situated on the skuzzy seaside edge of the armpit middle of Los Angeles County's erewhon, a beer bottle's throw from the wrong side of the Southern Pacific Railroad tracks, foghorn-listening distance from the Los Angeles Harbor, a piled-mile-high auto wreckage yard sprawled to the west, a marine salvage yard to the east, and to the north, not getting any prettier, ten square miles of stinky oil refineries and their Jupiter-sized oil tanks containing inflammables capable of burning alive all of Los Angeles and surrounds with only one careless wrist-flick of a match. Every night for the week, I'd been a fringed bikini-clad go-go girl in the raw, serving beer, dancing in the fire at The Fort, I'd wanted to run for my life but I couldn't because I had three kids to support, one of them a baby, after my husband left me for a Playboy Bunny.

Inside The Fort, up on the stage in the middle of the horseshoe bar, dancing away instead of Carlita, the sexy Mexican go-go girl who always wore a purple fringed bikini and usually danced there, twirled and jerked and bugaloo'd my boss, The Fort's night manager, Mick Jakson, singing along to the Rolling Stones' "Satisfaction" turned up so loud he'd not heard my commotion outside The Fort's door.

"And I tried...and I tried—" huffed and puffed Mick Jakson doing back-and-forth pelvic thrusts like hippies will do naked in a couple years at love-ins. Mick smiled and stared at his reflection in the ceiling-to-floor streaky mirrors on the walls facing him—very pleased with the good-looking guy he saw there in those big wide mirrors. The Fort's bouncers, two goal-post-shouldered, seven-foot-tall Samoan brothers guarded those mirrors with their canyon-wide bods from barstools slung across the room during barroom brawls (three in one week I'd worked there). Precious mirrors us go-go girls scrubbed smoke and beer off of every night after the bar closed, mirrors on three walls—and ceiling—that tripled the size of the place and the maelstromed amount of miserable, worn-out working men. Seeing The Fort empty of those stevedores, machinists, construction workers, oil wildcatters, bikers, and miscellaneous worked-stiff men was a strange surprise, like looking into an empty coffin you've dug up out of its grave (not that I'd ever want to dig one up). Mick turned to the right, to the left to catch sight of more of himself in the mirrors, overhead fluorescent lights making his teeth glow like little white Christmas lights. His eyelashes were long and black, like tarantula legs, and suddenly I realized he'd glued on false ones. Quite a pretty sight. I'd never seen a go-go *boy* before, and he was such a good dancer, I was enjoying his show so, I must've been smiling when Mick turned and saw me standing there below, watching.

"What the fuck are YOU doing here? And WHY ARE YOU LAUGHING!?" he screamed, covering the front of himself as if he were naked. Then, flinging his arms upward like a Nureyev who might fly away, he jumped, landed softly on his feet like a cat, a thump barely audible. He'd had some dancing lessons, that's for sure. And a lot of mirror-watching practice, too, because he craned quickly his chin to look over his shoulder at his backside, see how it looked in the mirror bent and posed like that. Looked great. He had cute, round, firm buttocks like perfect twin angel food cakes. Gracefully, but manly, like one of the Jets or Sharks in the movie *West Side Story,* he ran to the jukebox and unplugged the Stones— brrrt!—to say: "What the fuck are you doing here?"

"I work here, remember? Why's The Fort's door closed and almost locked? Where are all those thirsty men? Did you take some drug and forget to open up?" Mick Jakson, I knew, took a lot of drugs; he just worked here for the fun of it, plus the drugs.

"There's a riot going on! Don't you read the paper? Watch TV? A RIOT, man! In Watts! Los Angeles is ON FIRE! They've called out the National Guard!" Mick shrieked, sounding like a little girl. His hands shook while he kneaded them like two blobs of bread dough; he looked worried and tortured like one of those cowards or innocent men on Death Row going to the electric chair you see in the gangster movies. His pupils were dilated, too, and sweat glistened all over his skin, as if he were wrapped in cellophane. Oh, I finally got it: he'd taken some drug.

"A riot, you say? And you've taken some drug?"

Mick smiled, impishly. "Yeah. Some good stuff, too. LSD."

I frowned.

He waved his hand at me, dismissively. "You act like my mother." He said it to sound like "muh-thuh." I hated how people pronounced "mother" in those days. I loved my mother. "So what you going to do about it? Call the cops? Give me a spanking?" Mick was really a spoiled little brat: the rich kid of a rich man who owned muffler shops all over California and bought Mick that silver Porsche parked outside. "For your information, narc, if you are one, and Carlita thinks you're a narc, you're so square—LSD is not a drug. It's a mind expander." Mick stared up at the dirty-mirrored ceiling as if his mind expanded up there someplace amongst his cobwebbed, rain-and-smoke-stained reflection.

"I wish I were a narc," I said, meaning it. I longed for an ordinary, law-abiding, sober life.

"Well, in case you are a narc—" Mick stepped behind the horseshoe-shaped bar, poured himself a glass of foamy cheap beer from a beer tap, sipped half of it, then reached under the cash register into the dark cubbyhole shelf where cockroaches the size of chili dogs lived. I knew, because a big black cockroach had crawled up my arm when I looked in there for a flashlight night before last and saw a gun. Mick grabbed that same gun and pointed it at me. "Just don't try anything if you're a narc— Let this be a warning to you if you are—" Mick waved the gun around and bared his perfect orthodontia'd teeth at me like Bogart does in that old movie *The Maltese Falcon*. Then into the front pocket of his tight black pants he shoved the pistol so it would look like the hard thing he wanted it to resemble. Oh, Men, I thought. Playboy Bunnies, Riots, Drugs, and Guns. That's all they cared about August 12, 1965.

"I guess I'll go home," I said, and walked toward the door.

Mick chugged the rest of the beer. "You really don't know about the Watts riots?"

"No."

"You stupid or something? How could anyone not know about the riots?"

"I slept all day. I work the night shift, you know. I don't sub-scribe to a newspaper and my kids are gone with a neighbor on a camping trip so I didn't turn on the TV today. And I don't listen to the radio in my car because I want some peace and quiet before I get here to this noisy place." I was really getting tired of jukebox music blaring relentless Rolling Stones and live noisy blues and rock bands—the Rivingtons last week with their pa-pow-pow-pow-muh-muh-maow-maow-maow I had to listen to during my nine-hour shifts six nights a week. All that rock music was wearing me down in just one week. And I had a feeling I had miles to go-go.

"Guess you're not a narc. A narc would know about the riots. Come see, Babe, I'll show you the riots—" Mick took my hand. "The whole fucking world is coming to a fucking end! Wait'll you see—" Mick led me through the askew barstools, tables, and chairs, across the dance floor, onto the scuffed stage where the live blues and rock bands played every night, then through a door to a hallway to the hole-in-the-wall office to a secret door to a staircase and up to the flat, greasy, black-tarred roof of The Fort where guys in the band and their in-and-sin crowd hid to do drugs and drink whisky during breaks and after hours while they sat pow-wow on broken-down old furniture, their up-on-the-rooftop flophouse décor.

"The Penthouse," they called it. The size of twenty pool tables set side by side with a battered old coffee table covered with over-flowing ashtrays and glasses of half-drunk beer gone black with mold. Up there, we could see for miles north-east-south-west—the whole of Los Angeles wasteland, where all the dirty business of a big city took place. This was the pits, the janitorial business, the sludge scrapings off the sewage of all the odious vermin in the county, the mountain-high piles of trash, ash, smashed automobiles, trucks, buses, dead refrigerators, stoves, television sets, railroad cars, maybe some blood, sweat, and tears, too.

And dancing beyond all this wild pooh yonder was the fiery-fringed Watts ten miles away—as the buzzards flew in the distance—burning.

110

"Wow! Look at that! Isn't that the most beautiful thing you've ever seen? Isn't this FUN!?" Mick did a little dance, a jig, while shotguns and rifles and pistols and police and fire and ambulance sirens banged and whined and screamed in the distance as some men, and women, too, rioted, let it all hang out and do a little or a whole lotta shakin' mayhem, helping a city run amok. A jet airliner flew overhead, a golden rod in the setting sun, getting the hell out of town while a full moon came rising like no other, just like every moon ever born is like no other moon before and that particular moon was the L.A Watts Riots Silvery Moon, and it stared down at us with grand magnificent indifference and satisfaction for being faraway from the pyromaniacal crowd that was riot-making L.A.

"Wow—" Mick panted, patted his chest to calm himself, as the hot August 12, 1965 sun dropped behind the Pacific Palisades to the west of us and the sky turned royal blue and the horizon turned magenta, then blood red, the smoke from the riots' fires baking one of the most spectacular sunsets I'd ever see. Los Angeles can be so beautiful if, when, it is. Gazing at L.A. burning from the roof of the Fort, I giggled, a spark of latent juvenile delinquency inside my nerdy square self that had to admit Yes, indeed, and Wow, this really IS some kind of FUN.

"How about a quickie on my desk?" murmured Mick. "Better yet, on the pool table. We can watch ourselves fuck in the mirror. We'll be the last people on earth to fuck while the world comes to a fucking end." Mick pulled me to him to whisper tête-à-tête in my ear, to keep a sexy secret from the Watts Riots: "I'm a great fuck, Baby. Total sat-is-fac-shun, I guarantee it." He pressed the gun in his pocket against my left pelvis.

"Ugh," I said and pushed him away. "That hurt. I want to go home," I said and walked to the stairs that led back to the iniqui-tous, stinky inside of the inclement Fort.

"Party pooper," Mick grumbled at me, just as The Fort door rattled and then flung open, flashing twilight through the barroom. "Oh, shit," squeaked Mick when he saw two huge black men walk in. While they rubbed their eyes to get used to the dark, Mick pulled the pistol out of his pocket. "The Fort's closed, dudes! Get the fuck outa here, dudes, before I shoot your muthuhfucker asses!"

"What's happening, man?" asked one of the black men, huskily fine and mellow, no malfeasance in his tone. When he saw the gun, he raised his hands over his head. "Hey, man. We cool. We cool. Honest, man. Cool it."

The other black man, said, "Yeh, man. Yeh. We cool. We just came to see the Rivingtons. Put that gun away, man."

"LOOTERS!" Mick screamed. "RIOTING LOOTERS!"

"No, man. We paying customers. We just came to see the Rivingtons, man."

"LOOTERS!" screamed Mick, breathing hard, waving the pistol, his body twitching, his head jerking as the LSD suddenly overtook him.

I opened the door of The Fort for the men. "The Fort's closed, gentlemen. And the night shift manager here's just dropped some LSD. So better go home now."

"Sure, sure," they said and left quickly, ran through the gravel to their car, gunned the engine and roared off down the road.

As soon as Mick tucked the pistol back into the cubbyhole, its home amongst the demonic cockroaches, he screamed: "Look at the spiders!" He pointed at the mirrors of the wall and ceiling. He ripped his shirt off and threw it across the bar. He began to blubber, staggered to a pool table, crawled onto it and lay down as if in a bed, where he curled into a fetal position—his mind expanding, I supposed.

"I'm on fire!" he wailed, in agony, kicking billiard balls off the pool table onto the floor. For a second, I thought about telephoning for an ambulance to save his life, but he looked so stupid wallowing there, so willful, so skillful with this choice and not seeming to be in any real danger, seemed so practiced at this, I let him be, slammed The Fort door hard as I left, causing it to lock solid. Then

I made a fast crunchy high-heeled getaway in the gravel to go home, scary on the barren freeway as I heard sniper fire ping ping ping all around me, one bullet hitting and blowing off the off-ramp sign for the street where I lived.

Home, alone, I wondered what do you do on the night a city riots by the light of a silvery moon? I watched out my window for a while at all the smoke, listened to the faraway gunshots. Turned on my hi-fi and played my Frank Sinatra LP. "…Put your head on your pillow," Frank crooned to me. "What a lucky pillow…"

So I got my pillow, lay down on the sofa, and listened to Frank tell me how much he loved me, missed me, had me under his skin deep in the heart of him, had the world on a string because of me, needed one for the road because of me as I lay my head on a lucky pillow and thought about time and place. Thought about Fate of Geography. How we're dumped in places we don't ask to be to ride on chronological trains taking us to destinations we often do not choose. A pleasure trip for some, a rough road for others where some of us along the way must dance in frying pans and fire.

At least the ticket to ride was free.

Lucky me.

PAUL KAREEM TAYYAR

AT VENICE BEACH ON THE 20TH ANNIVERSARY OF THE START OF THE 1992 LOS ANGELES RIOTS, 1:30PM

This afternoon is a unicorn sun and the woman lying here beside me
Has not spoken in at least an hour
And the ocean is a jukebox resurrection of 60s electric stomp
That heroin-slides into my veins like a witch's spell
Like a police interrogation
Like a film scene of a violent assault that I cannot shake
Oh Rodney King you are playing on the flat screen television of the sky
And you are telling us that it's been twenty years
Since the burning of Los Angeles
See the skid-marks where your car slid off the race-ramps of the
Foothill Freeway
That look like the footprints of the dead
Like the footprints of Hansel-and-Gretel ghosts who disappeared
into the fires
Of Compton
Of Watts
Of South Central
Of Boyle Heights
Where white men with black batons and silver handguns
Shot out the full-moon fever lights of what-might-have-been
I am lying at the shoreline getting sunburn
Watching for mermaids rise from radioactive waters to bless the
children
Who saw their fathers burn down the record stores laundromats
pizza joints
Where their mothers used to take them
I am looking out for Atlantis rumors of federal money
To bring Skid Row back to life
I am watching as the Santa Ana winds drive a cavalcade of military jeeps
Carrying National Guardsmen who come bearing not tear gas
Not rubber bullets
Not industrial-sized flashlights that look down the alleys of a forsaken city

➤

And say it has nothing left worth saving
But instead come bearing drinking water
Electric power
College Scholarships
Soccer balls
And arrest warrants for slumlords
I am staring at the sea and looking into the imagined eyes of ten
thousand men
And women
Walking across the Sixth Street Bridge
White and black and brown
In dress blue uniforms and plain-clothes store-bought civilian ones
All of them holding hammers
Shovels
Water-buckets
Flower-pots
Cans of paint and farming seeds
Books of poetry
Acoustic instruments
And copies of the Bible the Koran the Torah *The Tempest*
      And *The Hunchback of Notre Dame*
Their eyes tell me they have come to rebuild a city that deserves their best
Their eyes tell me they have come to earn their children's faith
rather than to shake it

LeeAnne McIlroy Langton

MALALA YOUSUFZAI

Malala, you deserve more than this
More than a song dedicated to you by Madonna at a concert
In between her crotch shots and titty tassles

Malala, you deserve more than this
More women have read *50 Shades of Grey* and tried to
Recreate the sexual bondage of a young woman with their partners
Than have heard your name
Or your desire to be able to learn, to play, to love
You deserve more of our attention than that book does
 You deserve more than this

Malala, you deserve more than this
More of us know about you now that you have a bullet in your neck
Than we did when you had a voice in your throat
You deserve more

You deserve more attention than a few seconds on the evening
news

More attention than Beyoncé, Britney and all of the "real" house-
wives and Kardashians

combined

You deserve more attention than the new iPhone, the new yoga
pants, the new Ryan Gosling movie

You deserve more

From us

Our blindness to you is the reason that a man could believe

That a poem about a Grecian Urn is worth more than all of us put
together

CONRAD ROMO

HIGHS AND LOWS OF SILVER-TONGUED BASTARDS

"You ever broken down the word confidence?" Steve asks. "You *know*…its etymology?"

He's wearing a vintage red gabardine shirt from the fifties. The top two buttons on his chest are open and the ones across his paunch strain to not pop. *"Have we spoken about this already?"*

We're outside of a club in Hollywood getting some air. It's muggy, and I roll up my denim shirtsleeves. We know each other from a job we did ten years earlier. I was at the top of my game then.

"No, we haven't," I tell him. Loud rock music cuts through the walls. I'm having a bit of a crisis in my confidence. I've not made a sale in a couple of weeks. My thirst for blood isn't what it used to be.

"Well, 'con,'" he says, *"means…"*

"With," I say.

"With…yeah, that's right," he says. *"And 'fidence,'"* he pauses for a second, *"and 'fidence' is Latin for faith, trust, or belief."*

He looks away as if he wants his words to settle. He's Jewish and was Barmitzvahed and everything, but as an adult he's converted to Christianity. I have a feeling that he's going to ask me to get down on my knees and pray with him. I'd do it. Hell, I'll try just about anything to break my shit streak. His cell phone rings. He excuses himself and answers it.

I take off my hat and run my hand over my shaved head and wipe the sweat on my jeans. I think of a guy from AA telling me that Aramaic was the language used when the Bible was written, and in that tongue faith meant something like "knowingness."

I get Steve's attention and move my eyes towards the club to indicate that I'm going back in, and he gives me a hand signal to hold on for two minutes. I look at posters on the wall of the club advertising future performers. I prop one foot on a wall behind me and lean back. I close my eyes and try to remember a prayer.

Instead I remember back in the day when I had the touch and a Gary Larson *Far Side* comic strip taped on the wall behind my desk. In the comic drawing, there was of a guy in a suit and tie, standing in a sailboat, waving to a crowd of Eskimos on shore. They each wore hooded parkas and waved back as they stood next to brand new refrigerators situated outside their igloos. The sails of the boat are full and take the hero onto another conquest. The caption beneath the drawing said it all: "Worlds Greatest Salesman!"

That used to be me. Could sell sand to Arabs. Water by the river. Religion to the devil. But these days…

CONRAD ROMO

DAY IN THE LIFE OF
A SILVER-TONGUED BASTARD

Every day I get down on my knees and pray for a mooch. You know, the sucker, the laydown, the easy touch. There's a couple of different definitions for a mooch, but the one I mean refers to a person that can't stop themselves from the impulse to buy from every salesman that walks through the door. The desk or general vicinity of any mooch is always cluttered with every kind of imaginable shit that someone happened to be peddling in days past. Mooches are like sitting ducks, like fish in a barrel—like innocent little lambies come to slaughter. God bless them each and every one.

When they see you approaching, the little darlings get all excited. Sometimes they'll say something like, *"Oh no! Don't show me what you have!"* They'll turn their heads or hold their hands before their eyes, and they try to muster some will, they really do, and if they are resolute, they succeed for about nine seconds before giving in, taking a peek, then saying, *"Okay, what are you selling?!!?"*

I just love them! You *know* it in your bones the moment you spot one that whatever the hell it is you're selling, they're buying.

Every day, a salesman will go through a fair amount of rejection: everything from doors slammed in the face to various degrees of insults to security guards tossing their ass out of the buildings. So when you come across a mooch, oh, man, they are like an oasis in a desert of injustice. Justice being that every other door you go through should have a mooch behind it, but life is not fair.

Like the man said, "If you want fair, try Pomona." You know, the Pomona Fair? Anyway, mooches are beautiful. You come to really appreciate the little pecks on the cheek that life sends along in their form. And when they are in your crosshairs, when they raise their sweet little heads, for christsakes, don't overdo it. Let them live to see another day.

The guy that schooled me in door-to-door sales taught that there wasn't *ever* to be any *"cherry picking."* You know, only working certain offices (the "good ones"), while avoiding others.

In fact, every morning at our sales meetings before we'd hit the streets fired up and ready for blood, all the sales people would chant in unison, *"We sell people, not places, locations, or kinds of people!"* It's the right idea, really, if you're serious about getting the most you possibly can out of a territory. And, besides, you'd be surprised at the sales that will come where you'd least expect them. Now me, well, I've been at this so long that I can get away with it, the cherry picking I mean. Not you, though, or ninety-nine percent of you out there.

Remember: *"We sell people, not places, locations, or kinds of people!"*

When I walk into a building, I take in everything with quick glance: the security, the exits, and the names off the lobby directory. Then I head right for the elevator with a sense of purpose. I take note of where the freight elevator is, just in case. And if the security guard approaches, I don't get rattled. I'll just act as if I'm late for an appointment and put that into my walk, but I don't avoid him either. *Sometimes* I take charge and walk right up to the security and take the wind out of 'em by asking the time and maybe mentioning the name of a business I read off the directory a moment earlier to verify the floor. And what I say is more of a statement than a question. It's all in the inflection.

Then, I'm home. I just follow my feet like they're heat-seeking missiles. Like they're sharks drawn towards blood. I work with them like they are some kind of dowsing rod being drawn to water, and I let it happen. Don't fight the magic! Because that's what it is, making something out of nothing. *That*—the something outta nothing is the beauty of sales. I've learned to follow my whims. I trust that my feet know where they're going. I flow with the mojo. Light on my toes, I might walk past business after business then suddenly turn into an office.

Once my feet have done their job, it's up to my mouth to get to work. I read the room and play the idiot a little more or a little less, depending on circumstances. See, the minute people *get* that you are a salesman, they are going to expect you to come off with some smooth pitch. They'll instinctively brace themselves against the stereotypical snake charmer that they've seen before. The guy you've seen portrayed in a bunch of bad films. *This* is why playing the idiot catches them off-guard. See, to use a baseball analogy, they expect the hard and fast stuff, and you throw the off-speed stuff.

For nearly a year and a half, I made a living doing the dance in L.A, Denver, Boulder, Houston, Dallas, Chicago, and Milwaukee lugging a heavy custom-made black case containing shitty 8x10 framed art pieces. Calling the stuff art was a stretch—they actually were cheap foil etchings not much bigger than postcards. They had a quality about them that seemed to convey movement when light hit them the right way. They were cheap shit, but a lot of people liked them. I guess it's in the eye of the beholder. People just like boats, birds, flowers, horses, and old maps of the world, I guess. We had a little bit of everything. We used to say in part of the pitch that they were great conversation pieces, but I'm getting ahead of myself.

It went like this: you walk right into an office, or a nail parlor, or a bar. You don't knock or ask permission to enter. You just march right in and give your opening pitch. *"Hi I just came from next door at the (fill in the blank) and they got some of these and thought you might want some too. I don't know."*

The *"I don't know"* part was crucial to the pitch. Imagine me, dragging a three-foot-tall custom-made black case behind myself that held enough back up supplies for a selling frenzy, while in the other hand I held a couple of the art pieces concealed in a black pouch. I'd pull them out all in due time.

So, I'd make my clumsy entrance and give my dumb-shit opening pitch and then look around the office or wherever the hell I was, and act like I hardly knew why I was there.

If you play up this part right, it's like a routine they unwittingly fall into. You do your part, then step back. This, the reaching and withdrawing, is the essence of sales—though the majority of the mutts out there, the shit-heel salesmen of the world, will be stuck in the reach and *overreach* mode. Their sin is that they push and talk way too much. So remember that when I say step back, I *mean*, literally, step back. It's the beautiful part of the dance. The withdraw that gets them to reach for *you*. It works like clockwork. It's fucking amazing! Just do the opening pitch, look around like a dumb-shit idiot, and say, *"I don't know."* Then, take a step back and look around like maybe you're following a fly or some dust motes, or maybe you were just out for a walk admiring the surroundings and wandered into their place accidentally. And as if on cue, once you have withdrawn and taken a pause, they will reach as if they've rehearsed their lines by asking, *"What are they?"*

And then…don't answer right away…take a beat…before responding with, *"Excuse me?"*

And they will always, always come back repeating with a little exasperation, annoyance, or amusement in their voice, *"What are they?"*

And that is your permission, your turn to come back with, *"Oh these…I'm sorry…"*

And if there is more than one person in the office, they will almost always look at one another and try to suppress laughing right at you, because they will be amazed at your obvious stupidity, and **that** is when you *have* them. And, as if you had forgotten the black pouch in your hand, you discover it and pull out a sample and put it in their hands to get them involved, and at this point just go into the rest of your pitch and keep showing them what you have and the rest is basic product description, storytelling, and closing, and say, while nodding your head up and down smiling all the time, *"Aren't they nice?!"* And notice how they will nod their heads right along with you. Monkey see monkey do! The truth is that it doesn't matter what you are selling—costume jewelry, coconut trees, eel-skin leather purses, boxed meat, coupon books, or bad art—it really doesn't matter much what the product is because they will always reach after you have done the withdraw move.

I once had a woman who fell so badly for my dummy routine that she took pity on me and said, *"Oh, honey, you need some help,"* and then said to her office, *"Girls, come over here take a look at these."* And she did the rest of the work selling the goods for me.

Remember to keep an eye on the person who might leave the room suddenly or the hand going to a phone to alert security, and trust your feet to tell you when it's time to wrap up your business, collect your money, and get the hell outta there. But once you've got your mooch, you're in the money.

ELLARAINE LOCKIE

THE COST OF SOAP
Widowed at eighty-eight
he watched the buildings
on his homestead birthplace
slide into senility
Skin thinned on grayed wood
Walls stooped by snowdrifts and dust storms
Two-by-fours helping them
hobble into oblivion

He moved into town where he could
lean on accessibility
Tractor-towed his one-ton steel safe
Where he hoarded his non-belief in banks
with $80,000 in silver dollars

All his other effects trailed to town
except his father's 100-gauge shotgun
a pair of size eleven shoes
and seven bars of Jergens soap
That he just knew were taken
by a certain neighbor

It's the stolen soap that obsesses him
That daily demands atonement
at the hand of the town's sheriff
That crowds every conversation
he has at the Senior Center
➢

Even the silver dollars don't haunt him
like his mother's workhorse days
Spent outdoors stirring cast iron
cauldrons of lye and hog fat
While he and six siblings walked
around the edge of chemical burns

Until hours thickened the concoction
Days set it in molds
And weeks cured it into soap
in the homestead house
Whose weathered wood
has just been sold on eBay

LUKE SALAZAR

ALMOST EMPTY

The girl at Petco always flirts with me.
She tells of a guy who's there every Monday,
buys the same-sized one-pound bag of cat food.
When she asked him...*Why not a larger bag?*
he replied, *The cat is really, really old.*

I drop by my mother's house the next day,
and in her shabby, spotless kitchen, notice
that her refrigerator is almost empty —
contents whittled down to condiments,
baking soda, and a jar of maraschino cherries
there since my first ice cream party.

No food but what will be eaten this week,
and a tub of boiled chicken for the dogs.

Perhaps my mother foresees her estate sale,
cupboards emptied onto newspaper taped to the counter,
dollar boxes of unused cake mix and spaghetti,
and I hear her canny, cynical voice in my head—

Honey, no one wants to buy a dead person's food.

KATHY DAHMS ROGERS

SILVERFISH

What kind of life is this
sleeping between old sheets
in a cardboard file box
existing on paper and glue

Neither silver nor fish
scuttling away to hide their nymphs
wriggly wingless ugly bugs
condemned to lonely darkness

A common harmless pest
carrying no diseases
make no mess and do little damage
and then I see their eyes
their tiny compound eyes

IMAGE

It was easy enough
to look out my window and see
with imperfect eyes
a perfect scene:
A woman struck a pose
as she gazed at the Queen Mary.
She appeared to admire herself
in the silvered glass of the sea.
But we all know
that few things are what they seem.
When I look at myself
I see dust on the mirror.

KATHY DAHMS ROGERS

DREAMS

The streetlight shines so brightly
on the ocean, each wave has a silver lip.
That's when I realize how real
my Dreams are. Each day I awaken
to unbelievable news from unimaginable places
whose ghostly characters crowd out my thoughts.
I try to pin them down but they fade away
as Memory frees them to float over the bluff.
Each night I eagerly await my escape,
a better life, another dream.

MARCIA MEARA

SILVER SWIRLS

Silver swirls curve and gleam beside
Porcelain moons laced with ivy,
And roses red as a lover's kiss.
Firefly crystals sparkle, twinkle,
While violins sob in muted cadence.
Small flames dance on pale stems,
Warming the heart
But not the air.
Beneath all, a field of snow,
Crisp and starchy and patient.
Dinner is served.

MARY UMANS

SILVER STREAKS

Some people think they're better;
Some people think they're worse.
Some demean their fellow man
And rant and rave and curse.
Others live among the poor
With an open purse.

No matter who you think you are
Or who you think you're not
All will live and all will die
Don't let that be forgot.
As different as we all may seem
Our stories share a plot.

If you survive life's highs and lows
To live for many years
You'll get a mark upon your head
That may bring joy or tears.
The silver streaks in elder's hair
Proclaims we all are peers.

Resist the urge to rant and rave
Discriminate and blame
For silver streaks reiterate
We end up all the same.
The moral is be nicer now
We're pawns in the same game.

DANIEL McGINN

DRIVING HOME LATE

The moon keeps following our car
like a mute fish swimming
on a hook and a line.
In the passenger window you glow,
rain-frazzled hair, backlit
by halogen headlamps.

Your hand will not rest tonight
in my hand. The night slips away
speechless. Your hand continuously
shifts positions, tracing my veins,
exploring my fingers, reading my palm,
studying my skin like a book or a wall
in the blind night.

We've been driving for years.
I think to myself. I should tell you
I love you, shy, like the first time.

I keep my eyes fixed on the road.
I know about words;
words would bruise the moment
like a drunk pedestrian
stepping on the flowers.

MERRILL FARNSWORTH

MY ENCOUNTER WITH A FIERY OAK

Breathe! She shouted to me
as I walked beneath her canopy
of crimson leaves. Why do you hold
so greedily to one shallow
breath of life refusing to let go?
I know that once upon a time
life taught you to be still,
breathe shallow, play dead,
feign sleep,
a useful survival instinct
for possums, rabbits
and frightened children.
Look! It worked.
here you stand, half alive.
Breathe! She shouted to me,
take a belly breath
even if you must inhale
the poison with the pure.
Now exhale, empty out
your fevered lungs,
spew forth your dragon fire
as I take mercurial toxins
of lingering memory and fear
deep into my tangled roots,
reaching for quickened streams
of living water to baptize
every demon's breath.
Do not be afraid.
I stand beside you.
We are partners you and I,
breathing in, breathing out,

➢

no fear, no hesitation, no holding back.
You are not a small-voiced child,
a slinking possum,
or a rabbit caught in a hunter's snare.
You are a woman.
Breathe! She whispered,
a low branch brushing
tender across my cheek,
red leaves
dancing like dervishes
as I breathe autumn's fiery light.

JOAN JOBE SMITH

INNOCENT BYSTANDER

Here
in this Long Beach city
by the sea
seldom do we ever see
lightning striking
crackling electric silver fire
wicked witch fingers
fatal neon zaps across the sky
bandit blasts
from Beethoven thunder guns

and if we do see

it happens when
rain cloud winds
blow so hard
the ocean gets up
on its hind legs
and walks across the land.

PAUL KAREEM TAYYAR

THE DANCER DOWNSTAIRS

For Sherman Alexie

She was praying for rain, I figured. Swirling her arms like a helicopter falling to earth, her eyes closed like the dervishes I had seen when I went with my father to worship, her blue bandana the color of the stone on my mother's wedding ring. I don't know why I had such high hopes for her. It was July, after all, and it hadn't rained in months. But every afternoon I would look down on her from our dining room window, into the small apartment yard possessed of all the trappings of a sacred space: blooming flowers, a pair of lemon trees, a smiling sculpture of the Buddha, a bottle of wine on a simple wooden table.

I wouldn't say that I found her beautiful to watch. She danced too intensely for such a label. It was as if she were in some kind of trance, unable to pull herself from beneath the music's spell without the benefit of the safe word that some hypnotist had left without uttering. Even at seven years of age, I recognized the wildness of her movements as emblematic of someone desperately trying to get God's attention. I had seen it at the mosque in downtown Los Angeles that I attended with my father every Saturday evening, and again at the Holy Spirit Catholic Church that I accompanied my mother to the following Sunday mornings. I had even seen it in the alleys behind our building on Friday nights, when men howled at the moon after having stepped out of the Silky Sullivan's pub, their Army tattoos like hieroglyphs I was unable to translate. I knew this kind of dancing: it was employed not when the dancer was seeking joy but when she was seeking salvation.

"That's weird," Little Anthony said.

I hadn't heard him come in. Indeed, three months later, when Little Anthony and his parents would vanish, their apartment emptied only a day after I had spent the afternoon in their living room, Little Anthony and I watching a Lakers game on television, it seemed a fitting exit for the neighborhood kid who was something of a ghost. Big J., the complex's resident mayor, who dispensed nicknames with an authority usually afforded only to Indian shamans and Mafia dons, called Little Anthony The Phantom, because he was always appearing out of nowhere: a family would sit down to dinner, shut their eyes to say grace, and when they opened them, there Anthony was, asking somebody to pass the meatloaf. Two teenaged girls from Apartment D would begin to rub suntan lotion on their bodies while reclining out at the pool, and by the time they got down to their lower backs, there was Anthony, volunteering his services. In school, Anthony's seat would be empty for hours at a time, but whenever Mrs. Stark turned from her writing on the blackboard to survey the classroom, there he'd be, his hands folded on his desk, a big smile on his face. It got so you accepted the fact that Little Anthony appeared impervious to locked doors.

"What's so weird about it?" I asked.

"Who dances alone?"

"Lots of people," I said, hoping he wouldn't ask the obvious follow-up question.

"Like who?"

Damn. "I don't know. Lots of them."

"Yeah, well. She's not good enough to be dancing alone."

"I think she is," I said, defending her honor.

"Whatever," he said, already having shifted his attentions. "You've got to come see something."

I hated to leave her. In fact, it wasn't until Little Anthony had asked me to leave my post that I realized I had come to see myself as her secret sentinel, hew own private guardian angel. It wasn't just that I didn't want to leave her; I felt that I somehow *shouldn't*. And I had to admit, if she actually succeeded in delivering the rain, I wanted to be there when she did. Father Doyle was always talking about how the one thing he never understood about people was that they were always surprised when miracles occurred, and I didn't want to be one of those people. I didn't just want her to deliver the rain—if that was what she was seeking—I believed that she would. Besides, she was fascinating to watch: a melodic windmill trying to channel the surrounding energies to her mysterious purposes.

Of course, I followed Little Anthony out of the apartment.

"What do you think? Beautiful, isn't he?" Anthony asked, kneeling down and running his hands through the well-combed fur of what I assumed was a small German Shepherd.

"What kind of dog is it?" I asked, as I moved my eyes from the dog to the surrounding walls, all of them covered in the gang graffiti that was as much a part of the neighborhood as the persistent smog, L.A. Lakers gear, and *Dukakis in '88* signs. Years later, I would find myself comparing the abstracts on the walls of the Museum of Contemporary Art to the multi-colored petroglyphs that were all over my neighborhood, little phrases hinting at secret meetings, hidden treasures, acts of mystic prowess. Nicknames as wild as those contained within the pages of the Marvel comics that I loved: Earthquake. Flaco. Iceman. Priest. The Assassin. The Shah.

"It's not a dog," Little Anthony said. "It's a wolf."

My eyes came back to him. "Liar," I said.

"You're the liar," he responded.

"There are no wolves around here."

"My brother didn't get him from around here. He got him from his cousin in Tijuana. Paid him two hundred bucks," he said, his eyes widening as he recited the figure, which to us, who had never held more than a ten dollar bill in our hands at any one time, might as well have been a couple of million. Little Anthony's brother, who was seventeen and had dropped out from Los Amigos the previous winter and who had fathered three kids by two different local flacas, was always showing up on the block with stuff none

136

of us had ever seen: a loaded gun he had won in a game of poker, a pornographic magazine that we passed back and forth between us like the Ark of the Covenant, a small, sloppy cigarette with a foul odor that he swore had magical powers that would guarantee anyone who smoked it would never grow old.

"What's he going to do with it?" I asked. I still had not stepped up to the fence to try to pet the animal. I was a watcher in those days, not a participant.

"What do you mean? He's going to keep him."

"Is that allowed?"

"I don't know. But my brother said I had to promise not to tell anybody. Come on," Little Anthony added, gesturing towards me like the image that hung above our dining room table of Christ beckoning his flock. "Don't be afraid."

He opened the gates. I couldn't move. I stood rooted to the sidewalk, its pavement cracks like earthquake fissures that reminded us the world was always on the verge of cracking apart and swallowing us whole. After another ten seconds, I turned and ran towards home, Anthony shouting my name as I disappeared around the corner.

At dinner that night, my mother and I sat in front of the television eating grilled chicken, tater tots, and a basket of fresh strawberries she had bought on her way home from work at a local corner fruit stand.

In between sips of her water, she asked me, "What did you do today?"

"Nothing," I said, keeping my eyes on the television screen. It wasn't until having a son of my own would I realize that the defining characteristic of boyhood is one of a constant, enduring secrecy. You see yourself as an undercover agent constantly stuck behind enemy lines, unaware of who to trust.

"Nothing? Fair enough," she said, ruffling my hair with her hand and changing the channel with her other one. She settled on the news: Jesse Jackson was delivering a speech from the steps of the Los Angeles City Hall.

"Pay attention," my mother said. "This is one of the last great men in America."

After dinner, while the two of us washed dishes by hand in the kitchen, we heard the sounds of music floating up from the downstairs patio. My mother began to sing along to the song,

"Well she was an American Girl/Raised on promises/She couldn't help thinking that there was a little more to life/Somewhere else."

There, with the faucet running, my hands plunged into the dirty suds of a sink full of soaking dishes, I listened to my mother sing. It was the first time I could remember her singing outside of church, and her voice, now freed from the rigid acoustics of the cathedral's choir gallery, seemed to possess a beautiful recklessness that I had never heard in it before. She seemed to be singing not to reinforce a congregation's faith, but to reinforce her own. I almost didn't recognize her.

When the song was over, and my mother had turned off the faucet and had handed me a rag to help her dry the dishes, she said, "That poor woman has great taste in music."

I looked up at her. "She doesn't have any money?"

"It isn't that. She's very sick."

Though she sat me down and tried to explain the nature of cancers, which she said worked like the flock of evil birds in that horror movie I wasn't supposed to have seen but she knew that I had snuck off and seen anyway, I was still too young to fully understand what she was saying.

"But she's going to dance her way out of it," I said.

"What?" my mother asked, confused.

A few seconds later, we heard my father's tired steps on the staircase outside, and we walked into the living room to meet him, the implication of my response left dangling like the vanished love my parents had once had for one another.

For the next two weeks, life went on as it had. I would assume my position in the window to watch over the woman downstairs, and sometimes Little Anthony would appear beside me and ask me to come with him on some minor adventure: the Pac Man machine at the 7-Eleven was giving away free games and the owner hadn't realized it yet, or a fox had escaped from the nature reserve in Mile Square Park and a reward was being offered to whoever could find it. Other times, when the woman downstairs was finished dancing, sweat shining on her forehead like a benediction, I would return to my room to pray—always to Christ, who, given that both my Islamic father and my Catholic mother believed in him, cut down my prayer time by half—before heading out of the house to meet up with friends at the pool, hoping that afternoon would be the one where one of the girls would emerge from the water unaware that her top had come off during her swim.

It was a Monday night. Six of us: me, Little Anthony, Little Anthony's middle brother, Imperial Stevie, Surfer Dave, Blind Joseph (he wasn't blind, but deaf), and Felix the Stranger (we called him that because no one knew where Felix lived) all played a game of three-on-three basketball until long past dark. Felix had brought his boombox to the courts, and all night, as we ran up and down the court, we were soundtracked by the latest rap songs that Felix favored. Felix made six jump shots in a row from the top of the key, which convinced us that wherever Felix lived it was on the same block as God, and Blind Joseph stole a pass intended for Surfer Dave, took two dribbles, jumped from the free-throw line, flew into the air, pirouetted seventeen times, and then dunked the ball with all the authority that a nine-year-old kid could muster.

People driving by were so stunned by the amazing feats they saw that they called the police. When the cruiser arrived, out stepped a thirty-something African American officer with muscles the size of Texas on each of his arms. He climbed the fence, refused to remove his sunglasses even though it was almost ten o'clock at night, placed his thumbs onto the department-issue belt that contained a gun, a can of pepper spray, a flashlight, a baton, and a pair of silver handcuffs that made him look like the black John Wayne, and said, "Which one of you dunked that ball?

Imperial Stevie pointed at Blind Joseph. The cop stepped to Joseph. "You do that, son?" Blind Joseph didn't answer.

"Speak up, son."

"He can't," I said. "He's deaf." The officer nodded at me. He turned back to Blind Joseph and began to sign. He moved his arms with the kind of poetry that the woman downstairs used when she was dancing. I wondered if they knew each other. Maybe she had taught him, I thought to myself. Maybe he had taught her. It was one of those nights when anything seemed possible.

When the cop finished, Blind Joseph smiled, even laughed a little, and the officer gave him a high-five.

"Take care of yourself, ballers," he said.

Given that none of us could sign, we never learned what the cop said to Blind Joseph, only that every night for the rest of that summer, until Blind Joseph eventually moved away to the suburbs, the police officer would pull up once a night, roll down his window, and give us all a thumbs-up before speeding away.

With the game tied at 20-20, I caught a pass from Little Anthony on the wing. I hadn't been shooting well that night, but for some reason at the very minute I caught the ball I heard the music from the dancer downstairs begin to play, as if from within her walled garden a jukebox had come to sudden life. I let the ball fly.

It went so high that it hit the moon, denting it so badly that we wouldn't have another full moon for six entire months, and bounced off the belt buckle of Orion before falling back to earth and going straight through the net.

It was the first game-winning jumper of my life, and I wouldn't make another until my sophomore year of high school, when I would beat Santa Margarita with a bankshot from twelve feet away that the school priest would later say was a gift from God.

Little Anthony and I walked home together that night. "That weird lady is back at it again," he said. I didn't answer. In another five seconds he was gone, swallowed into the mists like a character in a fairy tale.

She didn't come out to dance the next day or the one after that. Without her there to fill it up with her energies, the backyard looked like an abandoned film set, or a staged site for a portrait painting that had never been completed. I sat at the window for the entirety of that second afternoon, unwilling to abandon my post. Once or twice I considered walking downstairs and knocking on her door, but I didn't. Young boys are only bold in groups, and for some reason that day Little Anthony was MIA.

My mother came home that night and said she had something to tell me.

"The woman downstairs passed away last night," she said, hugging my tightly, somehow aware that this was something that mattered to me.

It wasn't a decision I made so much as an impulse I acted upon.

When everyone had gone to sleep, I slipped open my second-floor window and jumped down onto her balcony. Her radio was still there, with an unmarked mix tape still in the sleeve. I picked it up and placed it into my pocket, climbed the wall, and began to walk down the street. I cut across Calle Independencia, slipping in between the used Fords and Chevys and the occasional Camaro that were parked all along the block, backed by the graffiti silhouettes that had been spray painted by unseen hands.

The world was full of ghosts, I thought. Men came out of their houses when no one else was looking to paint their identities upon the walls, and young women danced their way into a nothingness I feared I would never understand. At the entrance to Little Anthony's house, I slipped open the gate and walked through the yard, circling into the back where a small kennel housed the wolf. His eyes shone in the darkness like an angel's glittering wings.

"Come on, boy," I said, lifting the latch.

We walked through the darkness to the end of Brookhurst, crossed over to Warner, and climbed the chainlink fence and walked through the park. I found an empty place deep in the middle of the park surrounded by pine trees and wildflowers so tall they reached my waist. I kneeled down and released the leash that had been fastened to the small animal's neck.

"Find your way back to Tijuana," I whispered, as the animal turned from me and sprinted it into the sprawling expanse of a park from which I knew he would never be seen again.

I placed the radio on a small bench, slipped the cassette into the speakers, and hit play.

I began to dance.

MARGARET TOWNER

EMBROIDERY

I wear ethnic, Mexican embroidered
Flowers of urchin purple, scarlet,
With green vines bordering
The neckline; Indian gauze blouses
With tiny beads adorning the stitches,
Draped long enough to hide
My bulging waist and soft arms.
Yes, wear ethnic. Support communities.
Keep their art alive. Send my dollars
Where they are needed most. Wear ethnic
And indulge in the authentic.
I dress to show my alliances
To the world, the small knotted buttons
On my quilted coat of multicolored silk,
The necklace of seeds from a distant place,
Birds pounded into silver that peer
Through my tangled hair.
But I hadn't considered the hands
Until I saw the photo of the child,
The young boy leaning over cloth
Stretched on a wooden frame,
Reaching over the fabrics with a thread
And needle between his small fingers
To create my next purchase.

MARGARET TOWNER

FIFTH GRADE PROMOTION

The girls dress in turquoise taffeta
and wobble in silver high-heeled sandals
their long hair in curls cascading
down their shoulders, while the boys,
tall and short, grin in the line as they wait
for their names to be called.
Some wear tuxedos; nervously twist
their black ties, while others
wear tennis shoes, new jeans,
leave their shirttails out.
This is it. The end of elementary
school and the beginning
of chaos in middle school.
I congratulate each one of them
give them a hug, and shake
their parents' hands, while wishing
for the best possible outcome.
Only one thing I know for certain—
each of them can read.

MARGARET TOWNER

ON OUR WAY

The gentlemanly driver
with the silver hair
shouts out his memorized
monologue, more Spanish
than English, as we pass hotels
and theme parks, headed
to the Liki Tiki Village Resort.
He accelerates in curves,
jumps curbs, breaks branches
of tropical trees against
the windows of the bus,
stopping at drop-off points
to let vacationers out
of the unmarked shuttle.
I see a cardboard sign
by the side of the road,
between the Good Times Bar
and the Bargain World
Fun 'n Sun Gift Shop
—Let Jesus lead the way
to salvation.—
A woman smiles at him,
descends the shuttle steps
with a child on either hip
—Thanks for slowing down;
you were scaring my kids.—

CLIFTON SNIDER

NORWEGIAN WOODS

for Kjetil

You were dressed like a long Norwegian harlequin,
in shining black & silver you stitched yourself.
In the dark of the disco, I thought you were a blond
—dirty dishwater sort—not the redhead you are,
as Nordic as Erik the Red.

We walked across the street,
the rain stopped as if on purpose.
I mentioned Munch, you took me to
The Scream, painted on a building
like an announcement. Then
through the Royal Palace Park
with its dingy yellow & the weeping willow
growing out of the water. We cupped
each other's ass & kissed while a guard
stood stiff in the middle of the night.

You took me to your cold water apartment,
put on Barbra Streisand & lit candles,
like Norwegians do, as if to say
welcome, stranger no more.

...from *Moonman: New and Selected Poems*
(World Parade Books, 2012)

DALE SPROWL

MYSTIC MISTS OF ROTURUA

Roturua, New Zealand:
Couple dies of asphyxiation in motel on Fenton
Boulevard. They inhaled the sulfurous gas emissions
from the underground thermal springs of the town.

Chris, or Punatara, our 78-year-old Maori guide at the village of
Te Whakarewarewa,
spoke of her husband's passing nine months before.
Face wrinkled and covered with brown moles,
she told how he looked up
and the light in his eyes was like the sunrise
over the pink and white terraces
above the mists of Lake Roturua.
His face shone like silver,
like Moses's when he descended Sinai.

When the doctors wanted to restart his heart
with injections or paddles,
she said. No, you let him go.

She asked him, her husband of 50 years, who he saw.
She asked him, Is it your father? Is it The Father?
That is when he smiled and looked up.

She is lonely at night now.
After eleven, after the others have gone,
she goes to bathe in the geyser-fed thermal baths of the village.
Like in Eden, the Maori have no nakedness when they wash,
no male or female.
Now she unwraps her towel only for the hot mineral-rich waters
that flow under oceans from Icelandic glaciers,
waters heated by the volcano at Taupo.

DALE SPROWL

MARTINI?

I.

Tall, cold, and elegant I stand
unheld,
clear, sheer, and shaken
iced fire—

Within liquid invisible Stolichnaya and Boissiere

sits a lone green olive, pungent and pimentoed.

Shaken,

the olive trembles, quivers, questions.

Transparency reveals the rupture of vodka and vermouth.

II.

My crystal captures light and shadow,
silver grays, pulls in distortions,
swirls embedded in the unheld stem,
the sipless rim.

Succorless I stand—
shaken, not stirred.

➤

III.

I insist.

Stir me,

spur me,

move me,

choose me,

sip me,

drink me.

Be intoxicated by my love.

IV.

Without thinking, you reach out to grasp my stem.

Inadvertently, you knock me over.

Shaken before, now shattered and spilled,

the olive sits in the midst of the glass.

V.

Then I summon and muster the pieces,

and the shards rise, swirl smoke-like, fuse, reshape.

The cracks remain, seams, veins without blood.

The contents spilled.

The olive sits,

splintered,

and cannot fathom where the clear fluid has gone.

DALE SPROWL

FOGGY NOVEMBER

Mystic fog clung to air like film over eyes.
Unlike the usual silver tidal wave that strikes the coast,
it made the world invisible except for headlights and streetlamps
which created dusty pyramids reflecting nothingness.

The mist hung such that magical reality leapt to life—
a view of world one step back.

Sometimes veil of mist and shadow slows us,
and darkness, the uncertainty, reveals light.

AMY LOWELL

AUTUMN

All day I have watched the purple vine leaves
Fall into the water.
And now in the moonlight they still fall
But each leaf is fringed with silver.

WIND AND SILVER

Greatly shining,
The Autumn moon floats in the thin sky;
And the fish-ponds shake their backs and flash their dragon scales
As she passes over them.

THE BASKET

(Excerpt)

The inkstand is full of ink, and the paper lies white and unspotted,
in the round of light thrown by a candle. Puffs of darkness sweep
into the corners, and keep rolling through the room behind his
chair. The air is silver and pearl, for the night is liquid with moonlight.

See how the roof glitters, like ice!

Over there, a slice of yellow cuts into the silver-blue, and beside it
stand two geraniums, purple because the light is silver-blue, tonight.

See! She is coming, the young woman with the bright hair. She
swings a basket as she walks, which she places on the sill, between
the geranium stalks. He laughs, and crumples his paper as he leans
forward to look. "The Basket Filled with Moonlight," what a title
for a book!

BARBARA DAHL

SILVER THREADS AMONG THE GOLD

Gather round, children, and I'll tell you a tale of silver and of kisses: Silver Anniversaries that follow a kiss of commitment and thirty pieces of silver following a kiss of betrayal. We may find a moral at the end of this story. Or we may decide that morals are archaic or beside the point.

This tale begins when I was a girl of thirty, and heard that my boss took his wife to Europe to celebrate their twenty-fifth wedding anniversary. I told your dad that this should be our goal in eighteen years. You children would be on your own then, and the two of us could also celebrate our Silver Anniversary abroad.

I'd never before heard of a "destination anniversary"—this was even way before "destination weddings." Silver Anniversaries were then celebrated in a church basement with cake and little dishes of nuts and mints; coffee and lemonade were the liquid refreshments. But they were also a significant landmark back in the days when sudden heart attacks felled men and breast cancer ended many females lives in their forties.

In that era, divorce happened only in Hollywood, not in Iowa. I'd known of only three divorced people: a great aunt in the nineteenth century I never knew; your dad's sister who lived in another state; and the parents of a high school classmate—the only child I'd ever met whose father didn't live with his children. Divorce certainly wasn't likely to stalk us. Until it did.

It began on a Thanksgiving at home with just the six of us, just three years after that Silver Anniversary wish. It had been a bizarre spring-like day with temperature in the sixties. The roasting turkey overheated our house, and you kids preferred to play outside rather than come in and eat a heavy meal. After you were in bed that night, I talked to your dad about what we might do the next Thanksgiving. Perhaps we'd gather others whose relatives were elsewhere, like ours were; maybe we'd forego the traditional heavy meal for lighter fare, so we wouldn't be housebound all day. Or we could volunteer at a soup kitchen and eat with the clients.

Dad made no comments. After many unsuccessful attempts to get his input, a shocking fear hit me. "Don't you plan to be here next Thanksgiving?" I asked. He confirmed his exit plan, and I knew that he would not be going alone. She—our new neighbor who had pretended to befriend me—was married and had four kids also. The impossible was happening—to us.

I've since divided my life into "Before" and "After" the divorce. It's not that we didn't all survive this terrible time. But the memory of going through it is like what my father told me about people during the Great Depression. Even those who kept figuring a way to put food on the table during those years didn't know that they'd be able to continue doing it, he said, because they didn't know if the Depression would ever end. So those years have affected my decisions ever after, as the Depression did my parents.

Even you children don't really remember the "Before" me. Only two sisters, two cousins, and two lifelong friends have known both the "Before" and "After" me. Though I'm satisfied with my "After" self, the person I am now can be fully known only by those who recall all of my years. They are a drastically dwindling population.

Your stepfather is, of course, way in the "After" group, since we married when I was forty-five. We celebrated our Silver Anniversary five years ago, quietly, as we wished (no trips to Europe, no church-basement dinner).

Since then, your dad died following long years of dementia. At the point when you told me he didn't recognize your stepmother of thirty-five years, I'd ask whichever one of you I was talking to, "Does he still know you?"

What I also wondered was, "Does he still remember me?" I knew that demented patients hold onto memories from their distant past longer than more recent ones, and that first wives tend not to grow old in their original husbands' minds. That old song meant to envision a lifelong marriage is more fitting if the spouses divorce:

"Darling, I am growing old
Silver threads among the gold
Shine upon my brow today,
Life is fading fast away.
But, my darling, you will be,
Always young and fair to me."

So I wondered if and when I had been thoroughly erased from the memory of the man I had loved, who had divided my lifespan in two. It wasn't important, of course, and could not have been answered—or even asked.

You have made your own morals out of our story—or not. I'm lucky to have lived long enough to be grateful for and to acknowledge my own contributions to whatever life has dealt, and to cherish the person each of you has become. I have no wisdom about silver linings requiring clouds, or about my wish at age thirty being granted when I was seventy: a Silver Anniversary, untarnished.

(Barbara Dahl is the pen name of a Midwestern author. She has decided not to share this tale with her children—at least not yet).

MELISSA BERRY

SILVER VOICE

"Rickie Lee is in the pantheon of the greatest artists of our generation. She is an uncompromising visionary. It isn't always easy, but it's always worth it." RUSS TITELMAN, *GRAMMY WINNER AND CO-PRODUCER OF THREE OF RICKIE LEE JONES'S BEST SELLING ALBUMS.*

Los Angeles—October 6, 2012—Rickie Lee Jones, at the Broad Stage in Santa Monica, gave a compelling, rawboned performance that wasn't always easy to watch but certainly worth it. On the road to entertainment, the audience was unknowingly guided through a kind of catharsis with Rickie Lee and her music and stories, and her palpable connection with her adoring audience.

The Broad Stage was sold out for this performance and why wouldn't it be? It's a state-of-the-art space with plenty of free parking and amenities outside on the terrace. It's lovely. But even though it was sold out at show time, initially there were a few empty seats down front. The show was about to begin and was announced, but then we waited. And waited. Was it Rickie Lee?

They announced her, and then we waited at least another five minutes. The audience started to get restless so the management put on inane banjo music. Finally, after a twenty-minute delay and with the audience becoming audibly restless, Rickie Lee came onstage. There she was. Big, warm, lopsided grin, no pretense, she just came on stage as if she were coming into your living room.

She then started, after making mention of the empty seats. Expecting something from the new album, *The Devil You Know,* she opened very quietly instead with some old favorites. Not a particularly auspicious beginning. Only later did it dawn on the audience that she's a pro and was marking time waiting for stragglers to get there so they wouldn't interrupt her show later on.

Finally, they came in. She looked right at them and chided them for being so tardy, and we were right there behind her. We had been on time and patient, and now we were special friends with the "cool kid" on stage. The kind of kid you were forbidden to play with when you were little. The one that was exotically dangerous. That's Rickie Lee Jones. And that was the evening—exotically dangerous.

With everyone settled in, she commenced strumming and chatting with casually funny and spontaneous remarks, as she made sure everything was just right. She seemed so benign. She wasn't.

Rickie Lee's "Sympathy for the Devil" from her new album is an interpretation that would frighten Lucifer, Mephistopheles, and Beelzebub himself. When she finished, she was so delighted with herself because she knew she had scared the beejeezus out of most of the audience.

"Coolsville," from her first album in 1979, *Rickie Lee Jones*, sounded like a hip exorcism with Jeff Pevar playing an ominous organ background and her being all the characters. If her characters seemed like an ingrained part of her persona, that's because they are.

The co-producer on *Rickie Lee Jones* and *Pirates*, Grammy-winning Russ Titelman, described the scene when they were making *Pirates*, and it put much into perspective. "She was reading Rimbaud while she was writing the *Pirates* album. To me, she is like one of the Beat poets, able to create a world full of fringe characters who were actually her friends (a little like Tennessee Williams meets Charles Bukowski) and make them come alive."

We heard about the origins of this song as she was describing her early life in Hollywood. Her longtime friend Sal Bernardi, moving up to Hollywood from Venice Beach, Nero's Nook, porn stores and dildos, and eponymous names that follow suit. There was unrequited love and self-imposed celibacy with a sort of smirk knowing that the audience would be in on the joke. The Catholic Church, a priest with obvious and visible "sexual urge," and nuns with impure thoughts—she spared no one, especially herself. She sang about "watching heartbeats go by," reducing all people to just their commonality of a heartbeat and humanness.

During the evening of mostly ballads with Jeff Pevar on guitar and keyboards and Ed Willett on cello as her backup, they were all things to all people. Rickie Lee's sort of baby voice turned into a screaming banshee wracked with pain. Sometimes it was as if she were singing to herself while talking to the audience. And then sometimes singing to us and talking to herself. Pevar and Willett injected harmonies from some otherworldly place and made their instruments become whatever the song required. The three on stage were totally self-contained and Pevar and Willett were always expecting the unexpected.

The audience was like a group of pilgrims on some journey from Chaucer's *Canterbury Tales* or Boccaccio's *Decameron*. Trust was everything on this journey, where no one was sure what the destination was to be. There were the songs from *The Devil You Know*, and there were songs everyone was anticipating from over the last thirty years. This audience loved her and was happy with whatever she was doing.

The evening, which was seemingly short at two hours with no intermission, had a curious closing but certainly in keeping with the mood. After bows, Rickie Lee shooed Jeff and Ed off the stage and stood alone in front of the mike and simply sang "The Moon is Made of Gold," written by her father in 1954, the same year she was born. It seemed to be a lullaby to soothe us after our seductively tempestuous evening of otherworldly music and storytelling. But I'm sure no one in the audience went home and immediately fell asleep after this experience.

"One seed of humanity upon the burnt earth of inhumanity... will a forest find. There is only one devil. Do not be afraid of yourself." Rickie Lee Jones—*The Devil We Know*, 2012

Jackie Pledger-Skwerski

PASSING IT ON

We lost our only child, Peter, when he was thirty-four. For a long time, only black clouds hung over our lives; neither my husband nor I felt anything but grief. Now, however, we've discovered there can be a silver lining if one only looks for it.

Peter died early one Sunday morning, January 27, 2008. Cause of death was hypertensive cardiovascular disease, according to the County Coroner's report. The night before he died, he had hosted a going-away party to celebrate the graduation of a friend who had completed the Air Force officer training and was on his way to his first assignment. The party took place in our basement, where Peter had his design studio.

When the party broke up at two a.m., Peter was nowhere to be found. Dave discovered him in the computer room sitting in a chair beside the desk. Helen was with him. He appeared to be drunk, although everyone agreed he didn't drink much at the party. Helen and Dave suggested he go to bed, but he managed to say he was okay even though his speech was slurred. Then they offered to help him walk to the couch in the living room, but, as they tried to help him up, he slipped from their grasp and fell to the floor. He seemed very weak and had no coordination. Deciding to leave him where he was, Helen got a pillow for his head and Dave covered him with an afghan. After Peter drifted off to sleep, Helen and Dave sat with him for another hour.

When they were convinced that he had just passed out because he'd had too much to drink, they decided they could leave him. They thought he'd come to in a little while and go to bed on his own. So they went their separate ways—Helen to her parents' condominium, Dave to his apartment in the city. Peter was still lying on the floor, eyes closed, just like he was sleeping, when I discovered him the next morning.

Peter and David had been best friends since fifth grade. As a child, David spent more time at our house than at his own home. Their friendship continued through middle school and high school and college.

They didn't see much of each other while working toward their bachelor's degrees. Peter studied entertainment lighting design at Purdue University, and David studied technical theater at Ithaca College in New York. But when Peter went to California to work on his master's degree, David went too. They shared an apartment and took part-time jobs to pay the rent.

After completing their studies, they stayed on in California for two more years because they loved the location so much. They played Frisbee in the Redwoods, and Peter surfed a lot while David biked. Peter also started his career, and was very successful. But eventually they came back to Chicago to get permanent jobs and settle down.

That's when both renewed their acquaintance with Helen. She had been a year or so ahead of them in high school and neither of them knew her well. Dave saw her on Facebook and both were attracted to her and joked about their rivalry. But Peter won out, and he and Helen dated for the next three years.

We were all expecting them to announce their engagement. I had a sterling silver chain with crystals that had belonged to my late mother that I planned to give to Helen if and when they married. The chain had large sparkling crystal ovals spaced an inch or two around the chain. At the bottom of the piece, there was a lovely crystal teardrop. It was beautiful when the light danced on it. I had admired the piece since I was a little girl and imagined how it had looked on my mom as a 1920s Flapper. She had saved one flapper dress that she couldn't bear to give away, a silver one, although by now the silver sequins were tarnished. I imagined how she had looked doing the Charleston with those silver sequins dancing in the light and those gorgeous crystal orbs winking and blinking as she moved. Now, since the necklace didn't fit around my neck, I planned to give it to my future daughter-in-law, a much slenderer dark-eyed beauty.

The way the necklace sparkled kind of reminded me of Peter's chosen career as an entertainment lighting designer. He loved to play with light, but lately because of the collapse of the economy, lighting design jobs were almost nonexistent in Chicago. He made do with whatever work he could find.

Peter had been depressed because his career had come to naught after he had worked so hard to earn a bachelor's and a master's degree. He sought the counsel of a psychiatrist who prescribed antidepressants and anti-anxiety drugs. Peter also began to abuse alcohol, but he also tried to fight the addiction by going to Alcoholics Anonymous meetings.

Because of the alcohol abuse, every one at the party assumed his condition had been caused by something he had drunk or eaten or maybe had drunk before the party began. No one at the party suspected there was anything wrong with his heart and nobody realized his symptoms were similar to those that sometimes precede a heart attack.

It was nearly three years before the grief David and Helen shared blossomed into love. When it did, they asked my husband and me whether we minded if they dated and if we thought Peter would approve. We told them he'd be delighted and so would we.

For the next several months, they checked with us frequently on the progress of their relationship. Finally, they got engaged.

As they were planning their wedding, David and Helen decided they wanted us to participate in the ceremony and have some special status at the wedding. They christened us "Parents of the Couple," and we were listed as such on the program.

A year later, I found myself standing at the back of the chapel in the woods, waiting to be ushered to my seat. The day had been overcast and the grey clouds still hung over the outdoor chapel. Images crowded my brain. I relived the hour I had discovered Peter dead on the computer room floor, and how his dad tried to revive him with CPR. I thought about how he looked in his coffin with his long red ponytail fanned across the casket pillow.

There were also happy memories. What fun we'd had as a family scuba diving and taking a hot air balloon ride. And all of those family classes at museums where we learned to make kites and took water samples from Lake Michigan for the Shedd Aquarium.

We were so proud when Peter walked across the stage at Purdue to receive his bachelor's degree, and I recalled how he'd faced the audience and raised his arms in triumph. In California, when he received his master's degree, I cried tears of happiness.

My reverie was interrupted when an usher jostled me into reality, offering his arm and pointing toward the altar with his head. Once we were in place, the groom's stepdad sang the wedding song he had written especially for Dave and Helen. The bride then made her grand entrance on her father's arm.

I wore a corsage, ironically made of silver flowers. My husband wore a silver boutonnière, and we both read scripture. When the minister asked if there was any reason why this couple should not wed the "Parents of the Couple" stepped forward with the other parents and said "no."

Suddenly the sun burst forth through the black clouds. I smiled to myself knowing that it must be shining for Dave and Helen through the silver lining. Maybe Peter was peeking through the hole in the clouds, too.

The wedding was truly a joyous occasion. The bride and groom were so happy, how could we not be happy for them? Peter's dad and I also knew Peter was happy. Some grey clouds really do have silver linings.

It's been two years since the wedding and now we have a granddaughter, Hannah Josephine, born just weeks ago. When the pregnancy was confirmed, Dave and Helen drove thirty miles to break the news to us. "You're going to be grandparents!" they announced triumphantly. I haven't given Helen the silver and crystal necklace yet. I think this might be a good time. And someday our "granddaughter," Hannah Jo, will probably wear it too.

BARBARA ALFARO

CAR MA

Lucy Carlson drove along Ocean Parkway in a silver Sebring convertible with the top down, her mother beside her.

"I think it's rotten of you to only talk to me in this car," Mrs. Carlson said.

"Well, it's the one place I feel safe talking to you. I know how dangerous it is to get really angry when you're driving, so I feel sort of okay about letting us be together here in the car, like only meeting your ex-husband in a restaurant where you can't strangle one another during dessert 'cause people are watching—a *controlled* environment."

"You are hostile."

"Me? He shot every light bulb in the house when I left!"

"I always liked Charlie," Mrs. Carlson said. "He's so masculine."

"Mother! It's called misplaced anger. I could've been the next light bulb!"

"Oh, nonsense! He was just upset. He loved you very much. Look, Lucy—a Dairy Queen."

Lucy smiled. "Remember how Grandma always brought us ice cream when she came to visit. Dixie Cups. And she always wore that little black hat. Good God, Dixie Cups. I suddenly feel very old."

"Mama bought that same hat every time she bought a hat. She'd come home, take it out of the box, and ask Annie and me how we liked her new hat, and we'd say, 'Mama, you bought that same hat last year!' The same black pillbox hat with a short veil, every year."

"That little hat," Lucy said in a soft voice.

"Sometimes I think you loved your grandmother more than me. You always seem angry at me."

"I am angry at you."

"Why?"

"You know—the phone call."

"Oh, that. You mean you keep resurrecting my ghost simply because I didn't..."

"Simply because you told me Greg called me twenty years after he called! I bet you thought that was real funny. The twenty-year-old phone message. You would've been a terrible secretary. You ruined my life!

"Ruined your life? So dramatic!"

"You told Greg I had gone back to my husband and it wasn't true."

"He was too old for you."

"He was my heart...the other side of my soul..."

"Too old."

"The soul has no age."

"It wasn't your soul he was sleeping with."

"Intercepting someone's phone call should be a federal crime like opening someone's mail. You ruined my life. And all I can do to get even is not use your recipe for turkey stuffing every Thanksgiving!"

"Your loss. You know it's delicious."

"When I broke up with Greg, the last thing I said was, 'Don't call me again, unless it's with a marriage proposal.' He called, and you didn't tell me."

"If he was the one, why did you break it off?"

"Because I loved him, but he was only fond of me. I couldn't know then that his affection was better than most men's passion."

As Lucy stopped the car for a red light, an attractive man driving a yellow Corvette convertible pulled up beside her. She enjoyed the generous smile he gave her. The light changed and he turned at the next corner.

"A yellow convertible," Lucy began. "That was my fantasy when I was sixteen. Me, driving a yellow convertible and eating a bright red apple."

"Who was with you?"

"The apple."

"You're not getting any younger."

"I know my age, Mother."

Mrs. Carlson stood, extended her arms upward, and tilted her head back.

"Look, I'm the letter Y!"

"Will you please sit down!"

"Why? Why! The air feels so good!"

Lucy shouted, "Sit!"

"Woof!" Mrs. Carlson giggled.

Lucy focused on her driving. Mrs. Carlson stared at Lucy, then plopped on the car seat.

"You were always ashamed of me."

"Not always, Mother."

"Often enough."

"You were embarrassing. When I had the miscarriage, you brought beer to my hospital room. Cheap beer at that. Ma sipping her Reingold from a brown paper bag!"

"You would have forgiven Heineken in Gucci? I knew how much you wanted that baby."

"That was a swell experience. They put the failed moms having their D & C's on the same floor as the successful ones with their healthy new babies. Balloons, flowers, babies, cheer—and me and my ma with her beer!"

"Forgive me. I didn't care what the hospital staff thought."

"Not always."

"What?" Mrs. Carlson turned to her daughter.

"I wasn't always ashamed of you. It's just I wanted a mother who acted like the ones on TV. Donna Reed and Dixie Cups—Lord, just open my coffin now!"

"When were you proud of me?"

"Well, that time in freshman year of high school when the nun suggested I might have a baby out of wedlock because I was wearing nail polish. Remember, the very next day you marched right into the principal's office and let her have it, but good! It was like Jesus in the temple! Righteous indignation! I thought you were fabulous!"

"Such foolishness! And it was pink nail polish at that. Would the woman have told you that you were going to have twins if you were wearing fire-engine red? How warm it is today! I miss beer too. A nice cold beer with sausage and mustard."

"Ugh," Lucy blurted.

"And sex! I miss sex," Mrs. Carlson sighed.

"Sausage and mustard and sex! Quite an image," Lucy said in a mocking tone.

"You've got to stop!" Mrs. Carlson screamed.

Lucy hit the brake, and the car screeched to a halt.

"What? What is it? You scared me half to death!"

"Not the car! You! You've got to stop being so angry at me, you've got to…"

"Forgive?" Lucy pressed the gas pedal and restarted the car.

"Yes, Lucy. I'm tired of all this quarreling. I'm dead, for cryin' out loud. You are supposed to let me rest in peace!"

Suddenly, a small black pillbox hat fell into the front seat of the car right between Lucy and her mother.

Lucy screamed. "What the hell was that? A pigeon?"

Mrs. Carlson shouted, "You'd better stop the car!"

"Again?"

"Yes," Mrs. Carlson insisted, and her daughter pulled over to the side of the road.

Lucy lifted the hat very gently and without looking away from it, whispered, "All right! Damn it! I'll start using your recipe for stuffing this Thanksgiving!"

By evening, Lucy persuaded herself the hat had fallen from a passing truck. Yes, a shipment of hats headed for a millenary shop or department store and, somehow, one had fallen loose. Yes, of course, she told herself, that's what had happened. She kept the velvet hat with its slim band of embroidered roses and delicate veil on the top shelf of her closet, almost never noticing it, but always knowing it was there.

MERRILL FARNSWORTH

MY DIVINE COMEDY

I've lived my own divine comedy, or maybe it was a dream. Dante imagined his journey through the underworld all those years ago, now I imagine mine. Virgil the Poet was Dante's guide and did a fine job of navigating him through the various rings of fire. I am under the protection, such as it is, of a tortured playwright and a wry prophetess. Let me take you on a brief journey through my own personal hell, then, if you wish, you can show me yours.

My reoccurring dream of hell involves being somehow trapped in a world that is not real. I don't recognize anything and can't find my way home. I once had a nightmare some might call the American Dream. The location was suburbia. In my dream, circumstances forced me from my urban 1920s cottage to a newly constructed house in a pseudo-utopian village.

My distress at this move might be considered comedic due to the fact that my "real" home was plagued with numerous pesky imperfections. Some of the more obvious flaws: an earthen basement with spiders, crickets, and flooding issues, cracks in the plaster walls, and paint peeling off the outside trim. A highlight was an old tub with faucets that when turned counterclockwise to encourage the flow of water, then required repeated blows with a hammer (kept on the floor by the tub) to turn the faucets back to the "off" position. There were other annoyances that I seemed constitutionally suited to tolerate. One exception was a cold wind creeping through the kitchen walls each winter.

Back to my night terror…there were no monsters, rapists, or politicians, just an immaculate house with granite countertops, gleaming stainless steel appliances, an artfully open floor plan, and a perfectly controlled climate. The décor was tasteful. A well-intentioned home stager must have scoured numerous Pottery

Barn outlets, returning with every item I'd ever admired in the quarterly catalogues mailed to my old address. Had I been more astute with cardinal directions, I might have noticed the feng shui of the furniture. In contrast, all incidentals were strewn about with studied haphazardness.

The old cottage had been scattered with eccentric treasures from far-flung travels, as well as gifts from lovers and friends, and artwork created by cherished children. My hands gratefully received these treasures, whimsically placing each sacred object into the litany of my life. But here, in the dream house, not one knick-knack held a trace of my fingertips. And where was my family?

I needed fresh air. Each window was sealed shut to ensure an exact interior temperature of seventy-two degrees, so I opened the front door and stepped outside thinking to explore my new neighborhood. Bradford pear trees bursting with startling white blossoms lined miles of newly paved streets. The walk was pleasant, but after a few blocks a yearning for home overwhelmed me. I turned around thinking to easily retrace my steps. Each house looked the same. A trail of breadcrumbs would have been helpful, but I was no Gretel. Rows and rows of identical structures stood neatly before me. One of them had to be mine. Right?

After days and days of pacing up and down expertly edged sidewalks, I entered one of several taupe houses trimmed in white. A genetically blessed family of four was lined up at the kitchen island eating symmetrical entrées. As they glanced up at me, I mumbled an embarrassed apology, escaping before one word crossed their lips. I repeated this odious exercise, entering and exiting strangely familiar houses again and again. Soon I was madly crashing through identical front doors and slamming out similar back doors, working myself into a high-pitched panic. I jerked awake, barely able to breathe.

The crack in the ceiling above my bed was a blessed relief. I was home. Planting my feet carefully on the hardwood floor, I walked slowly to the bathroom, relishing each familiar step. The old clawfoot tub awaited me, stoic and stained with rust. Turning the tarnished faucets as far left as they would go, I stood back as steaming water rose to the rim. With the glee of a child finding her favorite toy, I picked up the hammer from the floor and banged ecstatically until the water stopped spewing. Sinking deep into the bliss of a hot bath, I laughed at myself for being terrified by a dream of a perfectly nice neighborhood.

Some years later, I woke up in a world that was unreal to me. It was not a dream. It was my life. I didn't recognize myself. The girl, sent home at age eleven by Mother Superior for violating the school's dress code with a mini skirt and black fishnets, was now a thirty-something woman swaddled in a floral dress designed by Laura Ashley. My compliant, underweight self sat in a church pew, insides coiled tight with unbelief, a handsome man gripping my hand with fierce hope I would keep my vow to love him until I was six feet under.

In my Laura Ashley life, sleep was only a dream. There was no appetite or curiosity. Stoic duty was my sole horizon. People and places that once gave me joy grew dim and out of reach. I had wandered into Dante's ninth circle of Hell where Satan was lonely and eager for conversation. He did all the talking, informing me that my beautiful dream of a perfect life was as empty as Cinderella's Disney World castle. Judas was there, making it clear I was in the Betrayers Club. Who was it I'd betrayed—my husband, my children, myself? Christ! *Yes*, Judas answered, looking pleased to have company, *you might as well get it over with now.*

The gossamer thread connecting me to every vow I'd ever made snapped under the weight of ambivalence. I was sucked into an abyss with the destructive power of a Texas cyclone. Everything familiar was destroyed in the spinning. Swirling in a dark funnel, pinned to a wall of sorrow, I gathered the courage to open my eyes. I was not alone. Ebony eyes blazed at me through a tangle of untamed hair. I locked into this piercing gaze with the total fragility of my being, surrendering to the alchemy of this shaman, this savior, this Madonna. All went black.

I survived the destruction of my dream and the breaking of my vows, but was undone by the memory of the beautiful, wild face in the abyss and the gaze of perfect love that broke my heart. I was cracked wide open and sucked inside out. What's funny as hell is that the cyclone spat me out in the middle of Tennessee, some level of limbo Dante forgot to mention.

With the languid grace of slow summer rain, a man calling himself Tennessee helped me to my feet, dusted me off, and asked for a cigarette. Lighting up, he looked me up and down, one eyebrow arched, and assured me I would often depend on the kindness of strangers. His traveling companion sported peacock feathers in her hair. She tossed off a wry comment about a good man being hard to find. They each seemed to consider the other highly amusing. Letting their wit sink into my bones, I traveled on with these two as my guides—Southern souls with a sense of the sacred and the profane, an eye for the misfit and at least a little sympathy for the Devil.

Perhaps like me, you are making your way through this divine comedy called life, never quite knowing what you are looking for but finding some good company as you tunnel your way toward light. I highly suggest depending on the kindness of strangers, laughing often, and choosing your guides wisely.

If you're lucky, they will choose you.

RACHEL CAREY

REFLECTIONS ON EAST 8ᵀᴴ STREET

She thought of her boyfriend—and she thought of him often—as a home, the kind filled with pillows and cats and warm cups of tea, so reliable you could curl up with a good book and lose yourself for hours. He seemed perfect when he wasn't depressed, and when he was depressed, that was nice, too, because it gave her something to do: holding him, cheering him, baking brownies. She felt that they could curl up around each other and pass an infinite lifetime together. Their first apartment after college was tiny, part of a small four-story walkup nestled in a row of townhouses in the middle of Alphabet City, with seats at each window and an incense burner and a barely functional stove.

So it came as a shock to her to see him outside one rainy afternoon with a look on his face that wasn't homey at all. It was eager, sharp, nothing like the sleepy sensitivity she was used to seeing. She was in a coffee shop buying them both hot chocolates on her way home from work when he walked past, his umbrella reflecting the silver sky, his face elated and keen.

She waited anxiously, desperately, for her drinks to be ready, then picked up the two thick paper coffee cups and rushed outside to follow him, spilling cocoa on her corduroys as she went.

At the corner he met and hugged a girl from his graduate program. She watched them closely from halfway down the block. It was a friendly hug, nothing beyond what was appropriate, and then she saw the two of them chat, nod, head down the block together. She followed and they entered a large old stone library, a branch of the New York Public Library system. But of course they were working on a project. Now she remembered. He had mentioned he might be late getting home.

She turned, unseen, and walked back to their place and sat down on the rug with her cat Grover and buried her fingers in his shiny gray cat fur. She knew, with a strange sense of certainty, that her boyfriend wasn't going to leave her. He wasn't going to cheat. He was going to return, that night, distant and sweet, and look over her shoulder to the world beyond her.

Her first decision was that brownies would not be sufficient. She pulled out of her cabinet all the ingredients for seven layer bars. Coconut. Chocolate chips. Condensed milk. Layer upon layer of sticky sweetness. She slightly burned them by accident, but that just gave the edges a nice caramelized quality. She put them out on a plate in the kitchen and said nothing about them when he came home at close to eight o'clock. She waited for him to go to the kitchen for his usual cup of tea—hoping he would say with shock, "What is this! Seven-layer bars?" and be in love with her again.

Instead, he emerged without a word and sat on the sofa and opened one of his course books, *Guilt and Psychosis in French Literature*. It was she who had been obsessed with Freud in college, but he who had turned to Freudian analysis in graduate school. She found this suggestive, in a Freudian way. Was he trying to outdo her? (Suppressed aggression?) Or become her? (Identity crisis?) Or was it just a requirement of his graduate program? She was working at a library during the day and studying library science at night, and most of her course books right now were on systems of preservation.

"Seven layer bars are in the kitchen."

"I saw."

"You don't want one?"

"I'm not hungry. Beatrice and I got a snack together."

"How is the project going?"

"Good, it's good," he replied. "We have a lot to do."

"I'll bet."

He looked down at this text again. "This assignment is ridiculous..." and he went on and explained what made it ridiculous, while she moved toward him and rubbed his feet. He smiled at her, and she had hope again.

"Hey," he said, "Beatrice invited us to a party out at her place on Coney Island. Do you want to go?"

"When is it?"

"Saturday. I was thinking I could head there straight from my morning yoga class, and we could meet up there. If you don't mind taking the subway by yourself."

"Yeah, sure. Of course. Taking the subway by myself," she scoffed. "Like that's so hard."

He didn't reply.

She got lost on the way.

Somehow, while her boyfriend was at the party of his secret crush, she was stuck on a J train from nowhere to nowhere, skirting the muddy outskirts of Brooklyn. She got off the train as soon as she realized her mistake, and stood there in the rain, crushed, and cried on the platform, because she knew she'd be at least an hour late. It was one of the few elevated train stations in New York with an open-air platform, and she could see the outlines of the city far away.

How could she have taken the wrong train?

Freud would have said she wanted to miss the train. Freud would have said she didn't necessarily want her boyfriend after all. This concerned her, as a Freudian.

But perhaps Freud would have said she was just testing him. That was a better possibility. She wanted him to worry. She was seeing if he would call to ask where she was.

He didn't call, so she got on another train to backtrack and try again. This time, she missed the stop.

How suggestive, Freud would have said.

"I'm just testing him," she told the Freud in her head, and she turned and at last, on the third try, got the right train, the right stop, the right exit, and stood blinking in the bright light of the early afternoon. Russians were everywhere, Russian food and Russian restaurants, and Russian writing was on the windows in stores.

She'd forgotten this was an ethnic neighborhood. To orient herself, she walked toward the beach, where there was a boardwalk with tourists with strollers and children heading to the Aquarium and little old Russian men drinking vodka in coffee shops at one p.m., watching her with the same anthropological interest she used in watching them.

She had to find Beach 2nd Street. She started counting down the blocks and wondered if Beatrice was Russian. A Russian spy fembot out to steal her man, wearing a cute canvas jacket and comfortable shoes to disguise her intent.

She arrived at Beatrice's building at last, and pushed the door buzzer. Beatrice sounded cheerful as she let her in.

"Take that, Freud! Didn't want to arrive here at all, you say?"

The lobby was covered floor to ceiling in mirrors with their edges painted. The whole lobby carried the distinctive feeling of 1965, glittering with brown and gold. There had once been a desk for a doorman, but now no one bothered to sign in the visitors. Packages sat there, unattended.

As she waited for the elevators, she stared at herself in the bright silver doors. She realized she looked terrible. A brown dress, yellow sweater, her hair in braids. She looked frumpy, older than her years, overweight, painfully shy. She looked like she had no interest in getting her boyfriend back at all. What would Freud have had to say about that?

It was terrible to see herself clearly. She saw her brown clunky shoes. She saw her thick yellow sweater over her dress, her thick tights. She saw herself as the cliché of the librarian grad student. Of course he wouldn't want her. She was the female equivalent of an old fuzzy blanket.

When Beatrice opened the door to her apartment, Beatrice was wearing an identical yellow sweater. Standing behind Beatrice with a mug of tea in his hand, there was her boyfriend, the same usual sleepy smile on his face sharpened by a keen awareness of—what? He smiled and greeted her and looked nervous at the sweater confusion. But she and Beatrice laughed it off. They shopped at the same stores, clearly. They were both wearing brown shoes with one-inch heels. They were the same, practically. Practically the same.

The party consisted of about five people and a vast spread of vegan food. Her boyfriend was a vegetarian, so she'd become one herself—but Beatrice, as a vegan, outscored them both.

Her boyfriend talked about the project. She watched him watch Beatrice.

Beatrice said to her, "Where did you get such a beautiful name? Dahlia. I love that name."

She said, "My parents were gardeners."

She walked into the bathroom, which had yellow curtains and brown towels. She looked at herself in the mirror.

Dahlia. She had always liked that she had an extraordinary name. She had wanted, as a child, to be a dancer or singer or actress, to be Dahlia Brown, name in lights, exotic as a flower on the New York stage. Now, looking at her braid and her hair and her quiet sweater, she felt anything but extraordinary. And what terrified her was not that her boyfriend was going to leave her, but that there was nothing she wanted to accomplish in her life that she could accomplish in a yellow sweater and brown shoes.

Perhaps she wasn't wearing this sweater because she was too frumpy to seduce her man. Perhaps she was wearing it because she knew he wanted her to be wearing it, that he liked girls like that. He had since college. No wonder he liked Beatrice. She was the female equivalent of an old fuzzy blanket.

When she emerged from the yellow bathroom, she told him she wanted to go home by herself. That she'd forgotten about a class. And on her way home, she stopped by a hair salon and cut all her hair off, leaving just a pixie cut. She bought new, shiny make-up and black clothes and high-heeled boots.

She returned to him that night transformed, shopping bags in hand, lipstick red and shiny.

He said, "Wow. You look good." He was surprised. They made love. He pretended, over the next few weeks, to be excited as she signed up for an acting class and told him she was dropping out of grad school in library science. He had a brief depression a few weeks later, so they talked a lot about his work, his life, how to help himself feel better, but nothing at all about her life, her transformation. She noticed that he carefully changed the subject as soon as she brought it up.

One night she got the letter in the mail. She had been accepted to an acting studio. Not the most prestigious one, but a good one, and they wanted her, Dahlia Brown. She took the subway uptown to his grad school to find him and tell him the good news. He texted her that he was in the student lounge. Could she find it okay?

The student lounge had a new, vast atrium of floor-to-ceiling windows, where students drank coffee and talked about books in a warm pool of yellow light.

As she approached, she saw him at a table talking with Beatrice. They were leaning in a bit too close. She waited for them to kiss, but they didn't. He was too nice for that, a nice guy, as sweet as a warm cup of cocoa. She knew that as soon as she broke up with him, he and Beatrice would be a couple, that they would be good together and nice to everyone, and everyone would like them.

What would Freud have said about her, standing out in the dark like that, watching him watching Beatrice? She didn't care. She felt sleek and dark and free.

She stood outside for a long time and watched them, watched Beatrice, this eerie reflection of herself, this future that could have been hers. It was like watching her life go on without her.

She would have to break up with him that very night. She knew it for certain. She walked away into the nighttime, the warm light of the college café growing dimmer and dimmer on her high black heels, and disappeared like a cat in the dark.

KENDALL STEINLE

CERTITUDE

A walk seemed like the right thing to do.

A man in a long wool coat was trudging ahead on the parkway.

A math book somewhere would see the situation as a word problem waiting to happen: How long will it take the girl walking at such-and-such a pace to pass the man in the long wool coat walking at such-and-such a pace, and for how many nanoseconds will they walk exactly in step? Moreover, when will the train speeding south-by-northwest traveling at such-and-such-too-fast-pace hit and kill them both?

I always liked math. But since I was never good at it, I fixated myself on employing an irregular gait, a personal attack against a greater evil. Long step, short step, long step, pause, two quick. I acted like a normal human being taking a stroll when I passed him, then pressed on. The path curved to the left and then the right, and then there was a bench, and I sat down.

The only sound I could hear was my own breathing and then the sound of the random snowflakes drifting here and there as they joined their fallen comrades on the terrain, though they really didn't make a sound at all, so I had to pretend.

I didn't bother brushing the snow off the wood, and my rear was immediately cold and wet, but at that point it was already too late. I was already sitting.

I dug my elbows into my knees and let my face rest in my palms, staring intently at my shoes. I pressed my left foot into the snow then raised it, letting it hover while I analyzed the zigzag pattern imprinted in the snow. I analyzed for some time.

The man in the wool coat approached.

He paused a moment in front of the bench before sitting next to me. We made eye contact for a few seconds, then broke off. There was darkness to peer into.

I sat there in silence next to the man. Once or twice I thought about saying something, like hello, but then advised myself against it. There was nothing to say. So I kept quiet.

"Because it's really hard," said the man after some time.

I waited for a response or a follow-up. When nothing came, I asked, without looking at him, "What is?"

He just stared off into the distance like people do, in silence. I shuffled my feet once more and began analyzing another footprint.

He stood. He shrugged his shoulders and tucked his chin into his chest, the collar of his jacket becoming a fortress against the cold. His jacket was long and black. That's what happens in the winter at night: everything is dichotomized between the blackness of the night and the whiteness of the snow. All that's left, all that can't force its way into the blackness or whiteness, vanishes into the grayness with flashes of silver and light, then fades into the noth-ingness, like a star burning out. He lowered his jaw as if to tighten the wall of wool, as if to speak.

But he didn't. I looked up at him and nodded, but I didn't say goodbye.

He nodded back and turned, and I watched him walk away. His hips moved only slightly under his coat, and he kept his shoulders hunched in his departure; the cold would never reach his neck with that sort of posture. I bet his shoulders ached something awful in the morning.

I waited awhile, imagining I had some sort of pensive look on my face. When I tired of pursing my lips and narrowing my eyes, I relaxed my face and stood up. I shuffled back along the parkway, pretending the snow was crunching under my feet because that's the only sound that's fitting when one details walking in the snow. I walked over the bridge and paused at its peak, resting my elbows on the rail and trusting the wood with my weight.

The water, like the sky, was black. Dichotomy. It trickled over the rocks, reflecting the moon in momentary glimpses of silver that were immediately lost almost the minute they appeared, because the silver just wasn't strong enough to make it. Its brief flashes of existence could not confine to either end of the spectrum, and vanished entirely.

I cleared my throat and rested my head on my arm, watching the stream. Water always seemed to have a sense of what was going on; it appeared determined, it had its shit together, it knew where it stood and knew where it belonged, it knew of all dichotomies and feared none. You never saw water stop and turn back around, stop and change its mind. When it jumped, it jumped with conviction, and it never looked back. If it did retract, it usually had a purpose or a good enough reason. Water had focus, a place to go, it was acutely aware, and it knew what the man was talking about, even if I didn't.

Being alive.

KATI THOMSON

YUMYUM

When the sheriff is done with her, Mama picks up my book from the mattress and sits down to tell me Russell is gone for good. She says it isn't my fault, but her eyes flit to the corners and creases of my little room. They catch on long shadows stretching across the wooden floor and the window curtain swaying in a rare breeze. I know she searches, despite herself, for Yumyum, who she says isn't real.

I glance to the alcove under the eave, where Yumyum's poured himself like a quart of oil across the top of my little white dresser. He lifts his head out of the sulky puddle he's made and blinks button eyes that show no remorse. I turn back to Mama, whose own eyes are red and puffy from crying, and I know it isn't my fault, but it's close enough.

"I didn't see it coming, Ruthie. I never would have let him… It's better anyway, just the two of us." She tells it to the tissue she's tortured into a ball and is now carefully picking apart, as if returning it to its proper shape will put everything else back together. Misery rolls up hard and dense behind my bellybutton, about the size of a lemon.

"Do we gotta move?" I ask.

"Not for a while. I have a little saved," she says, lifting one side of her mouth into something like a smile. The lemon in my stomach knocks around so that relief won't make me forget how bad Mama feels.

This place hasn't been any better or worse than anywhere else we've lived. White paint on the outside of the house dirtied into gray a long time ago and is shedding to show more gray of the weathered wood beneath. My attic was cold and drafty in February, and now it's almost too hot to breathe up here.

The neighbor lady, Mrs. Farley, doesn't like us much. She glares at me from her side of the hedge she's always trimming when

I go out in our scrubby yard. But her sister, Miss Luella, keeps a bunch of cats, and one, a ginger, climbs the tree into my window every afternoon, laying claim to me.

The kids on the block think we're crazy for living in this house because they say it's haunted by a lady who chopped her husband's head off with an axe and then shot herself dead. They informed me of that, stopping me in the street one night like a bunch of dogs sniffing me out. Then they rode their bikes off and have stayed away ever since. They were right about the haunting, though I brought my own ghost.

It's just like every other place I've been to, but six months in one spot has made it familiar to me, and that counts for something. And I need to be strong, because something needs to be done about Yumyum.

When Yumyum is happy, he shimmers. Arms and legs and chest and head, brimming with heavy liquid moonlight. That's when he's quiet and peaceful and won't give any grief. He smoothes himself across my pillow, satiny and cool against my cheek on a summer night. He weaves himself into the cloth sleeves of my winter coat and holds me tight when we go walking. He barges down the hall like a noisy Portuguese Man-of-War, dangling a tendril for the ginger cat, just to make me laugh.

"Yumyum…yumyum…yumyum…" His words don't make any sense, but they rumble dark and smooth like chocolate on my tongue. They warm my insides like the rum Mama put in my bedtime milk when Russell started coming over. They make me feel not so alone.

Yumyum likes old music with violins that don't have drums or any words. It's hard to find it for him because the stations 'round here don't play much but country and Mexican polka. When we moved here, he got excited because I found an old wooden radio in my attic room that worked. Guess he figured since it was old, it would play old music.

I turned it on and spun the dial for him, but all it played was the same old stuff, only cracklier, plus a bunch of gasbags talking about baseball and politics. The air in the attic stopped still, heavy and waiting, as Yumyum's temper drained his silver away until thunderclouds boiled across his face, and I had to duck the storm. The lightning bolts he spit out knocked my cardboard boxes against the wall. They broke open, and everything I owned dumped onto the floor—including the one framed picture I have of Grandma Louise, who's dead now. It's the only thing I'd grab if the house was burning down and I had to run. I got mad, too, and bawled a little. Yumyum blew his storm away and pulled a long face to show me he felt shameful.

When I wouldn't forgive him, he cried and moaned, throwing himself this way and that around the attic, like a fly caught in a window. That didn't work, either, so he disappeared for a while. When he came back, I felt a lump in my pocket that turned out to be an old peppermint hard candy with dirt and purse lint stuck to it. I ate it anyway, and it was the best thing about that day, since I got in big trouble for Yumyum's mess and didn't get dinner that night.

I guess Yumyum liked Russell at first because he could play the fiddle. Mama brought him home one night from the dry cleaner where they worked. His job was to take all the dirty clothes out of those big rolling canvas bins and throw them into the washing machines and then move the loads to the dryers. You'd think they'd walk in the house smelling good, after working in a place where they wash clothes all day. But the sourness of other people's bodies rubbed off on them more than the detergent, and they both looked damp and smelled like armpit. Russell ducked through the doorway and peered in, the way tall people do. He had fine eyes that smiled with his mouth, and he looked at my mama as if she was a miracle from God.

She pulled him into the kitchen as if she had an apology ready if things didn't go well. I felt sorry for her, gauging my reaction, as if I were the decider in the house. But that's the way it always is: Mama watches me and I watch Yumyum, who'd muddied himself into a crackling cloud of no-good above them. That is, until Russell showed me the thing he'd brought with him.

"Your mother tells me you like fiddle music," he offered. Yumyum stopped his squalling. "After supper, I can play a little if you like."

My ghost snapped himself back into shape and eyed the battered case that Russell set carefully by the coat rack. Mama and I sighed in relief, and, like a sunrise breaking through morning fog, the air lifted in the little kitchen. She went into motion, getting Russell settled at the kitchen table with a bottle of rum and a Coke, darting from fridge to stove, checking the skillet to see what dinner I'd started.

Russell poured a drink and pulled out makings for a smoke. I watched his long fingers sprinkle tobacco into the thin paper.

"You like it here?" he asked, eyes flickering up, waiting for me to speak.

"I like it fine," I said, squirming under the attention.

"What grade you gonna be in this year?"

"Seventh." I glanced to Mama. It was a question. I hadn't gone to school much.

"We've been talking about homeschooling this year. Right, Ruthie?" she said over her shoulder, moving chops around in the skillet.

Russell flipped open his Zippo and lit his cigarette. The paper flared and hissed into a neat little ember as the tobacco caught and he drew deeply. It smelled good. He picked a shred from his tongue and blew the smoke up toward the ceiling, away from my face.

"Are you a smarty pants, then? Too smart for them teachers here?" He said it the nice way. I sat back and smiled, made shy.

"Oh, Ruthie's smart, all right," Mama said for me. "You should see all the books she has up there."

"Well, she don't say much," Russell said. "She's keeping all that smart stuff to herself." Tapping his temple. "Well, that's all right, Ruthie."

It felt good in the kitchen, right then. Like one extra voice made it a party. Even if no one said anything for a minute, it was still noisy with people. It felt so good, I forgot Yumyum for a dangerous moment, but he was glued to Russell's violin case. He poked at its latch with one misty finger, tried to get his hand inside, then lashed out when he couldn't do it.

The noise of it falling on its side made us jump and Miss Luella's ginger cat darted up the stairs with a growl, taking the blame. Yumyum's eyes saucered, but silver was still skimming across his skin. We laughed a little and it broke up the dread in my throat. Dinner passed, quick with breathless chatter. Mama stood to take the dishes and Russell reached for his case.

Yumyum followed it to the table with hungry eyes and gave a little moan of pleasure when Russell opened it up. Even in the bald light of the kitchen, the wood grain shined deep and lustrous. It wasn't just a fiddle—it was a *violin*.

"It was my grandpa's," Russell said, lifting it to his shoulder. He drew the bow across the strings, making a screechy sound. Yumyum looked like he'd been slapped.

"Just kidding," Russell said. "I'm not the fiddler Grandpa was, but I can play a few tunes."

He began playing in earnest—a low, mournful song full of smoky mountains and dark hollows that made Mama lift her hands from the sink and turn to watch. After the first true notes, I held my breath, helpless, as Yumyum wound himself around the strings like blissful threads of silver, letting Russell's bow set him to vibrating with the music. It wasn't classical, but it slipped painful and sweet into the space around my heart like nothing I'd ever heard. I was captured, and so was Yumyum.

We clapped hard and laughed when Russell blushed pink, and asked him for another. He played the next song well enough, but it wasn't as good. Yumyum peeled himself from the violin, looking peevish. To my horror, he wrapped himself around Russell's head and whispered in his ear. Russell's bow skittered across the strings, dropping the folk tune he'd been working on. Then, as if crashing off the road into the woods, he scratched out nine notes in an entirely different key.

Yumyum flung himself against the wall, a noncommittal pearl gray, watching Russell's face with his otter head cocked to the side. My heart hammered out a painful staccato. Russell would know something was terribly wrong here. He'd storm out, unsettled and angry without understanding why. I prepared myself for shouting and the rattle of glass when the door slammed behind him. But he just dropped his bow and scratched his beard.

"Hunh," he said.

Oblivious, Mama handed me a mug of hot spiced-up milk and whispered it was bedtime. I said my goodnights, limp with relief, and made sure Yumyum drifted up the stairs after me. He gleamed, plump with silver again, rumbling in satisfaction.

So it was my fault, everything that came after. I should have remembered his greedy, needful heart and warned Mama. But my silence made me his accomplice. My silence and my childish yearning for better days. That night I slipped willingly into sleep, dreaming rum-softened dreams of kitchens filled with music and laughter.

THOMAS KUDLA

THIS GRAY HAIR MEANS SOMETHING

This gray hair means something. I'm sure you don't know what I mean, at least not yet, but you will soon enough, once I describe how these gray hairs represent more than old age, how only battle scars gained in fierce wartime fights could at the most nearly compare to these gray hairs, how I earned these gray hairs. Every last one of them. I don't pretend to be wise. I certainly am too immature to be considered old (and, of course, my age is not even half that of the average man's mortality, not that I pay mind to such statistics). This has been a short life in time thus far, but I'm hoping to make it last longer. I've already lived a full life, seeming much longer. If you don't believe me, then look at these gray hairs. It's not heredity; it's psychology.

I was eighteen when I noticed my first gray hair. Actually, it wasn't me that noticed. My girlfriend, my high school sweetheart at the time—she noticed that gray hair. That single gray hair wandering from the center of my scalp, as if aware of the wars fought inside my mind, sought refuge in the escape toward the sun. Lying there, our eyes entranced with that shining orb's setting motion in all its variegated splendor, she brushed her petite hands through my hair. She always loved how soft my hair was—"for a guy." We watched that sun sink deeper toward the earth, and we talked about many things—I discussed my parents' impending divorce; she told me about how happy her parents were together. I mentioned how sad I can get sometimes; she said she smiles whenever she feels that mood strike her, and it changes everything. Then she found it—that gray hair.

"You've already got a gray hair," she said, her dimpled smile and light voice hiding her judgment. "You work too hard. You stress too much. Someone your age shouldn't have gray hairs."

I laughed it off and kissed her. I kissed it away, all my fears about being too serious or being too sad or being too dysfunctional or not being enough for her or being too much for her. I kissed it away. She reciprocated my kisses in innocent pecks, naïve to the reality of where those gray hairs came from. She thought she knew. But I knew better.

I earned those gray hairs during my seventeenth year of life. One day, an alarm woke me up and breakfast was served. It smelled so fresh and so tasty. Eggs, pancakes, syrup, coffee, orange juice. Everybody in the family was talking, most of them saying dreadful things about me. I ran downstairs to catch them criticizing me. Laughter as I approached. Then nothing. No eggs. No pancakes. No syrup. No coffee. No orange juice. Not even a single family member awake to greet me. It was 4:30 a.m., and I was going crazy. Those negative voices flooded my mind as I realized something had short-circuited in my brain. Something was not quite right. I ran to the living room, the one room where hardly anyone ever went. Maybe no one would be there, maybe the voices would stop in there. They continued. And now the breakfast smells came back. I've never done hallucinogens, but this was some bad trip.

Days went by like this. Familiar voices once friendly had become my enemies. Things were in slow motion. I could not react fast enough in real life because months and months of worlds and worlds were playing countless moments and moments throughout my mind. My brain wasn't working properly. While I was hallucinating another life, a fearful, threatening life, caught up in delusions about what was going on around me, my friends and family and teachers and peers saw how truly lost I was. They searched for answers. Was it a brain tumor? Was it brain damage? What happened to him?

While they anxiously sought answers and some sort of resolution, I feverishly navigated my way through a nightmare of dying family, cruel friends, and mistaken identity. I did not know who I was. I did not know who to trust. I created delusions to make sense of the hallucinations. None of it made sense. I tried to make sense of what makes no sense. It drove me mad. Years later, I would tell a psychotherapist in precise detail what each of my hallucinations and delusions were, including possible interpretations for them. He told me to not bother; rarely, if ever, does it make sense. But I felt like I could make sense of it. It all came from my brain, I thought, so surely I could decipher whatever frightening and disillusioning code this was, esoteric and scary, real scary.

It took me almost half of a year to start living a normal life. It took a diagnosis and all sorts of drug combinations—trial and error, of course—to finally break free from the madness. I left school for a while just so I could get better. This madness would enter my life time and time again, like a storm that was never truly gone. We tried to predict it like meteorologists try to predict storms, but it turns out psychologists and psychiatrists are less precise and accurate than meteorologists. I suffered through more of these bouts; I have even more gray hairs. Every single one of those gray hairs reminds me of the sadness and madness that held me captive for so many months, so often in my life. I earned each of those gray hairs. They are scars. I'm a survivor. This gray hair means something.

COLLEEN DELEGAN

THE LOCKET

The sun bore down on Elizabeth, the heat radiating through the thin fabric of her bonnet. The hem of her ratty skirt swept the dirt path as she looked along the road for a strong branch she could use to thread under the handles of the buckets she would fill at the stream. Finding a sturdy piece of wood, she took the trail down to the water, careful not to trip over the bulbous roots that occasionally surfaced like angry snakes lying in wait.

The current was docile today, with just enough movement to provide evidence that it knew where it should be going. She sat on the bank and took off her shoes, pulled off her socks, and hiked up her skirt. She dropped her hot feet into the stream, audibly exhaling as the cool water lapped at her legs.

She noticed a miniature hill made of small stones close to where she sat. She guessed it was probably made by her younger brother, Adam, who often came to the stream to amuse himself. She hated to ruin the child's pyramid but felt entitled to have a little amusement herself. So she beheaded the top of the hill and swiped a small handful of stones. One by one, she tossed them into the water. First she heard the playful plop, and then she watched the concentric circles growing larger and bigger as they spread out, then communed with the current and completely disappeared.

Her daddy often thought she was a bit *off;* he hated the fact that she enjoyed moments like this, watching the circles she generated by throwing stones into a stream. But, most of all, he really hated when she drew pictures for Adam. She told her father that her dreams were so vivid she felt compelled to create pictures from her lush imaginings. But daddy flew into a rage and told her it just wasn't natural to make drawings of foreign thoughts one had at night. He threatened to tell Preacher Jeremiah what she said, but then decided against it. His concern was if they proclaimed her crazy, or, worse, possessed by an evil spirit, they would take her from him, and there wouldn't be anyone at home to take care of Adam. So she wised up. When the embers in the fireplace cooled down, she collected tiny pieces of charred wood and stashed them with a small sack of soft red berries from the woods. Then, when Daddy and the other men went off on their hunting trips, she and Adam secretly made pictures. Truth be told, even though Elizabeth believed her father didn't like her drawings, she believed more strongly he simply hated her for looking so much like her mother. She noticed there wasn't one picture of Justine in the house anymore. Not one piece of clothing in the cupboard, not one trace that she had ever existed. Elizabeth was sure there was some significance that her mother died on Elizabeth's eighth birthday, save the fact that it gave her father one more reason to hate her.

Elizabeth gently moved her feet back and forth so she could watch the translucent fish zip around her legs. She laughed as they slid across her skin, forming perfect figure eights in the water. She leaned back on her elbows and closed her eyes. She wished she could take off her bonnet, her dress, her petticoat, her corset, her slip, and, finally, her bloomers. She imagined plopping into the stream, experiencing the freshness of the water and the momentary freedom as her teenage body slipped under the concentric circle she saw herself making.

For a moment, she was nearly joyful, as this simple exercise made her forget her obligatory chores and the omnipresent dry heat that awaited her return to the farmhouse. She grabbed a new handful of stones and continued to toss them until she felt something irregular in her hand. A small, square locket, barely discernible through the dirt, nestled in her palm. She turned it over a few times, trying to make out exactly what this unusual piece of jewelry was, but it was covered with mud and tiny fragments of dried leaves. She took the underside of her skirt, dipped it into the stream and gently rubbed the necklace. Little by little, a tiny silver book was revealed. With shaking hands, she found the clasp and popped the locket open.

☽

THE SORCERESS

He was so preoccupied that he hadn't noticed the seasons had changed and the girls had all switched to their pretty summer dresses. Fringed dresses that brazenly grazed mid-calves, stylish bobs, and smart ankle shoes replaced the heavy fur-trimmed coats, and the long shawls women were sporting from the month before. Normally, he would have noticed, but now he was concentrating so hard he didn't feel his feet slapping against the cement, his irregular gait mimicking a drunk's. Mothers pulled their small children in another direction, his look was ominous and his complete focus disturbing.

He crossed Michigan Avenue, which was made of freshly laid bricks, and stepped into a long, narrow alley that wound behind the shops, behind the city center. He took a set of stone steps down a level, emerging from this labyrinth; he was thrust into a different side of town.

He followed the river for a few minutes, shaking his head in amazement. The famed reversal of the waters, now flowing from Lake Michigan westward, seemed to be working. There hadn't been an epidemic in years, a reality his father didn't live to see.

Where the river jogged to the left, he turned right. The streets were dusty except when a person opened a window and threw out a bucket of dirty water. The unlit walkways were littered; no one cared to pick up trash, leaving it behind for the scavengers to take—whether it was of the larger, two-feet, or smaller, four-feet, variety. The day's laundry dangled from ropes lassoed between buildings, maids were returning from their jobs lugging sacks with leftovers pilfered from their employers' houses. A young man loosened a horse from his cart. He dismantled a "Tin for Sale" sign that hung between two poles radiating upwards from a high seat. As he worked, the lines of metal plates and bowls banged and clanged in dissatisfaction.

At the next dirt road, he turned right. The small house existed only when you knew where to find it, only when you needed to come there. He was never pleased to go to home, but once he walked up the path to the door, he was happy to leave the burden of, the insincerity of, and the terror of, all that came before.

He heard her voice before he saw her face. "Oh, Adam," she said pretending she was surprised to see him. "I've just put on a new pot of coffee. Come into the kitchen and sit."

"Hello, Elizabeth," he said. "You look well today." He stuck out his cheek as she brushed her lips across them. She turned and walked down the hallway.

He slid off his shoes and hung his hat on the pegs by the door. He took off his coat and shook it slightly, trying to get rid of the worries that clung to him as tightly as the brush burrs did when he ran the dog through the meadows.

He didn't bother to ask how she knew he was coming, somehow she always did. Inevitably, she would have the table set perfectly with food at the ready. Today was no exception.

As he walked into the kitchen, the smells mingled and wrapped around him like a large chamois cocoon. The sweet smell of freshly baked cinnamon rolls, the pungent coffee, the blooming flowers on the windowsill, and the musty odors from the larder, all formed a nostalgic cocktail that nearly made him forget his purpose.

She poured the coffee in one graceful sweep. He took a cinnamon roll and set it on the plate in front of him, not sure if he was even hungry. He looked up and saw the framed picture over the sink. It had wrinkled from age but he still could make out the child's handprint made from smashed red berries, but the color had faded from red to pink and the charcoal signature was smudged. He stared at the picture until the sound of the coffee pot hitting the metal burner jarred him back to the moment.

He didn't turn around, but he felt her presence. Elizabeth pulled out a chair and sat down as if the weight of her body suddenly had become too much for her skeleton to hold upright. Adam took a sip of the hot coffee, pretending not to notice that it scalded his tongue. Stoically, he took another gulp; this time, the burning was so intense that the nerve endings in his mouth went numb. He kept drinking the coffee until it was finished. He set the cup back into the saucer.

Justine walked around the table like a hummingbird that was not sure where to land next. She continued to circle until her mother put out her hand and touched her arm. As if commanding an unspoken order, she sat down. Adam looked at her, and was not surprised to see she looked radiant. Her hair was lustrous and pulled up into an old fashioned chignon, belying her youthful age. Her cheeks flushed as she spoke.

"Uncle Adam," she said. He put up his hand to silence her. Elizabeth visibly recoiled at this gesture but said nothing. The girl instinctively put her hand to her throat and nervously played with a silver locket in the shape of a book, which hung around her neck.

SYED HAIDER

LETTING GO

In the shady depth of life
Are the lonely nests of memories
That shrink from words.

Rabindranath Tagore

On Friday, May 25, Memorial Day Weekend, during takeoff, the left engine of a shining silver DC-10 separated, flew up and over the wing, landing on the runway. The crew struggled to control, but the left wing stalled while the right wing continued to provide lift. The plane rolled onto its left side, crashing into a field, wing first. All (272) passengers and three people on the ground were killed in that crash. Miriam Berg, twenty-two, May graduate, journalism major, University of Chicago, died in that accident. Light of Ashok's life, inamorata, his ladylove. He was twenty-five, and that was twenty-five years ago.

After the crash that killed Miriam, Ashok contemplated suicide but instinct to survive kept him going. Life force invisible, soft, and silent, like that current of water that moves underneath the earth's rocky labyrinth, that feeds plants through capillaries enough nourishment to sustain it, where life seemed impossible.

He looked away every time someone would mention that crash, he'd not hold eye contact for that conversation. He thought that pain would never get less and it will never be dull. On the outside, he seldom appeared in doubt or in particular anguish; no one saw him cry. He put his sorrow away until he was alone. He grieved in private. He felt as if he did not have the right to mourn in front of others. Nobody knew his pain and sorrow.

Ashok met Miriam during her freshman year; the year he graduated, Bachelor of Electrical Engineering. After four years of courtship, he knew that she was the one for him and he knew that she felt the same way about him. Now that she had graduated and had a job at ABC News, they decided to live together. The night before the crash, they'd had dinner at Peter Lo's, Chinese food. They made love in the candlelight and slept cuddled up in his bed that night. It rained intermittently with loud thunder. She slept through it; he didn't. The morning was sunny and cool. On the way to the airport, they listened to Springsteen's, *Greetings From Asbury Park, N.J.* on a tape..."Blinded By the Light," "Growin' Up," "Mary Queen of Arkansas"...*It's not too early for dreaming...*

At the airport, she kissed him on the lips, whispered, "I love you." She held his hand and said, "See you in three days." She picked up her carryon bag from the back seat. "I love you," she called out again. "I you too," he said and watched her. She wore a light-blue silk dress with deep purple flowers and a long olive-green gabardine raincoat that made her look taller. She waved and walked away to the departure gate to catch her flight to L.A.

After hearing the news, Ashok wanted to disappear, move away somewhere, where no one would know who he was and what had happened to him.

Time passed, fate or whatever that governs the life, *Samsara,* the ever-turning wheel—the cycle of birth, death, and rebirth, continued...at age thirty-three, Ashok married Sita. He loved her but never fell in love with her. Sita soon learned that she had married a damaged man and accepted her fate. They had two lovely daughters, but, after all these years, Ashok felt broken and hollow, and he often reflected on his life and what it could have been with Miriam.

Come November, beyond the period of time set by the pope, in which forgiveness of sins is granted in return for acts of repentance or piety. Twenty-five years after Miriam's death, past the Silver Jubilee that was all blue and grey but no jubilee, Ashok visited Shanti, India, the village of his birth.

There was loneliness in his being that he could never get rid of; he had never told anyone, friend or family in Shanti, about Miriam or her death. The secret part of his being that nobody knew, Miriam, *his second self, a friend that sticketh closer than brother.* His American life, his American life of twenty-five years ago.

Sylph n.: An elemental soulless female being imagined to inhabit the air.

There was nothing to say.

Like the tin man in a silver space suit, satiated with loves possessed and lost love, filled with the shouts of devotion and echoes of doubt, morphed into elated and defeated cries. Ashok strolled towards his childhood friend Ali's house, talking to himself. A crescent moon followed him, and the nearby red and blue glow of a funeral pyre shot above the wall of the cremation ground. Stench of burnt flesh filled the air.

In November, one can see life for what it is, barren and still. In November, one can see the skeletons, the bare bones, arid fields, and naked trees. We are all born to die. On the other hand, life can be an accumulation of denials. Let's see what is ahead, let's look in the past, but let's not be where we really are.

Miriam once told him that he was the first man she'd heard urinate. Once he stood above the white ceramic bowl, sounding like a wild mustang. In a short time, the thunderous rain ceased, becoming the sound of a slow shower, then a minor drizzle. For a while, out of embarrassment and courtesy to others, he took the toilet paper and wiped the rim of the toilet bowl. But it became too much of a chore, like a tired old whore, now he sits down on the toilet seat, peeing a trickle for a long time, breathing slow. "I'm getting too old," he says to myself, "to benefit from the wisdom that comes with age." And God knows it is not easy, but a man does what he must. Just being best, the Gold medal, not Silver or Bronze, was good enough for him.

The coolness of his lonesomeness burned inside of him like dark peat fire gone out on the surface yet smoldering inside. Ashok walked on, missing Miriam, wishing to find her one place or another. In a heartbeat, the moment passed. In the blink of an eye— it was life, and it was death. She will never pass this way again. She is gone for good. It is a desolate, unadorned, unrelenting thought. Twenty-five years, the Silver Jubilee, should be plenty of time to put to rest, to forget, "a forget-me-not," to overcome a love lost, to accept and get on with it. Life is meant for living, move on and live. Here is to killing me, and here is to the part of me that has died and gone away.

The burden of mind is to explain everything, but feelings are feelings. One feels before one has developed a purpose. One feels without cognition, one feels un-egotistically, and totally self-indulgently. Explain and expand your ways of thinking. Contemplate, but do not commit to agony or sorrows. Change your outlook. Put in the happy thoughts, wear a happy face, smile and make promises. November can be one evening; you wake up the next morning and it's spring again, green sprouting renewal of life. I am, I shall be, because I live, because I feel. I sense a sad and lonely tomorrow. But maybe, he says to himself, just maybe, I can repent and accept my regrets, say no to heaven-sent sorrows. File them next to the years of remorse and regret. Say no to soul-burdening parasites that lurk in my heart…live and be left alone. "Give me a sign," he cried out. "Show me that Miriam was for real and not an object of my imagination, *whither goes the dew*. Don't let my appeal die without response."

The crescent moon followed Ashok to Ali's house. He knocked. No response, but the door was ajar. He walked in, but there was no electricity. After Ali had lost Batool, his life companion, his wife of more than twenty-five years, he locked up all the other rooms of his large house and moved into the living room. He slept on the floor on a cotton mattress. Ali sat on a prayer mat saying *Isha* prayers. An oil lamp burned, placed on the floor. His long silver and gray beard glowed in a dramatic fashion in the dim light. The living room had the same old Persian rug and the same old teak sofa with blue and gray cushions from way back when. Ashok sat down on the sofa and waited.

Ali got done with his prayer, looked up, and said, "Ashok, you look in pain."

"Dear Friend, a lot has happened that I couldn't explain."

"I know," said Ali, "last night Miriam visited me."

Ashok couldn't believe what he'd heard. Did Ali say "Miriam?" He said nothing.

Ali picked up the lamp and adjusted the flame. There was additional luminosity. "When in distress, I find a great deal of solace in abnegation of self's will by seeking the will of God," said Ali, his voice calm. "Sometimes a man is deprived of certain material comforts or encounters the loss of a loved one, so his endurance, trust, and faith in the will of God can be tested. Man has no choice but to accept the will of nature. I'm in habit of meditating; it makes me more accessible to the Creator. One could ascend to heavens, beyond the state of space and time. Last night, after performing the ritual ablution. I said the supererogatory *nafal.* This worship is *mirag,* a ladder, ascension, beyond here and now. I sat on my prayer rug. Lightening flashed, and I felt an effective presence of Allah, and during that brief moment, I felt enlightened and inspired. It was at twilight. The transfiguration took hold of my soul. I saw, felt, and said things I hadn't been capable of before. I visited Miriam or rather she visited me. She was not suspended in the air nor did she have wings. She was like you and me. She stood by the doorway. She wore a long olive-green gabardine raincoat, and a light-blue silk dress with deep purple flowers. She told me that dress was your favorite. A message was communicated between our spirits. And she wanted me to convey her message to you."

A Jewish woman appeared in a Muslim man's consciousness to convey a message to a Hindu man. Taken aback to learn that Ali was so enlightened, Ashok sat there, stunned, overwhelmed, and stared at Ali, an expression that was half wince, half smile masking his face.

She spoke softly and said, "I was blessed to have met Ashok. Our time together was short, but it was love of Rhada for her Krishna. And we were absolutely marvelous." Her message to you is: "Life floats upon the current of chance and change. At the end of our journey, we need to let go, reach within, and claim our remembrances. Ashok doesn't have to look back to get a glimpse of me. I'll always be by his side. He needs to relax, be receptive, and he'll feel my presence."

Alert and focused, Ali looked at Ashok for a long time. He concluded. "All this was made known to me through divine inspiration. After my state of enlightenment passed, I was back to being who I am, your humble friend." Ali smiled. He looked pious and virtuous.

A current of cool breeze blew in gently from an open window. Ashok sat there confounded, happy, and sad. There was a sense of relief, like Miriam was real then and again now. How did Ali know about Miriam, Ashok wondered. It does not matter now. In believing such happenings, one negates one's pride, but not one's person. *Life floats upon the current of chance and change. At the end of our journey, we need to let go, reach within, and claim our remembrances.* Leaving Ali sitting on his prayer rug, Ashok walked out, back to his father's house, the house that once was his home.

VICKIE LESTER

ON A SILVER PLATTER

What happens when the once-young bride of an aging movie star approaches thirty? In the case of one Harvard dropout (and former au pair), the bride found herself at the USC School of Cinema-Television—tuition paid by court order—separation in effect, divorce pending. Sitting in a darkened classroom, the former au pair, Billie, discovered her favorite film opened like this, a close-up on stenciled letters (all caps) spelling out "Sunset Blvd." on a leaf-strewn curb...

Head credits scroll on asphalt as the camera rolls down the street. Tilting up we see a wide boulevard lined with trees, hills rise in the distance. In the halftones of five a.m., glaring motorcycle headlights crest the pavement. Police cars race by in an affluent neighborhood and make a turn down a private drive to an old estate. The police pull up and came to a stop at the stone-flanked entrance of a mansion. Men in uniform run up the front steps, most split to the left and move with urgency through the garden to the side of a pool followed by photographers toting cameras with huge flash attachments. A man in a suit is sprawled face down in the water. His arms are splayed. His legs hang lifelessly from his hips.

Looking up from the depths of the pool, please picture the corpse, a young man, striped tie pulled slightly askew, mouth lolling open, eyes staring. The police and photographers crouch and lean over the water to get a better view. A sardonic narrator who has been commenting throughout ends the scene with a disembodied, "The poor dope, he always wanted a pool, well, in the end he got himself a pool—only the price turned out to be a little high."

On hearing this, Billie let out a blurt that sounded somewhat like a laugh. It wouldn't be the first time she identified with a fantasy, a dark one, but a fantasy nonetheless.

The dissolution of marriage, though far from final, wasn't falling Billie's way. She no longer had a pool. When her son wanted to swim, he had to go to his father's. The marital home near Coldwater Canyon Park had been sold and the court was holding the proceeds in escrow. Billie was living in a duplex on Doheny, walking distance to Kate Mantilini's, a restaurant with the dubious distinction of revitalizing the meatloaf. Her BMW had been downgraded to a Renault. Does anyone remember Le Car? Her attorney advised forbearance; the longer the case went on, the better her chance of prevailing. However, Billie found her Hollywood friends, the "wives of," were spooked by her plummeting status. With the exception of a group of young ladies who had also once taken care of the children of the rich and Hollywood mighty, they all had stopped returning her calls.

Over months of weekends, and an inestimable amount of Chardonnay, Billie's old friends rallied. On one such evening, Billie, lapped by the nostalgia wine can bring, said, "You know who I miss? I miss Natalie. Remember her? She was the older one who came to the park with her little half sister...Wasn't she like ten years older than we were? You know, I've met her dad, he runs that, that, Para-who-see-what's-it-studio...God, I'm drunk. She told me not to marry that, that..."

One of her pals, topping Billie's glass, paused for the word to come, but what issued forth from Billie with a incantation almost inhuman was, *"Che mentire that fucking old bastard, pezzo di merda, mi malediranno, HO maledetto, e il suo la puttana, dalle mie labbra l'orecchio di dio."*

"Whoa!" said one.

"What the hell was that?" asked another.

And another looked around the room, under the throw pillows at her elbow, glanced over her shoulder, and then insisted, "English, please. Or should I be burning sage?"

"It's just something I've heard people say," Billie demurred.

"Christ almighty, what people? People with pitchforks and pointy tails?"

"I don't know." Billie shook her head. The wine sloshed back behind her eyes. Her hangover was going to bite. "Does anyone know where Natalie is these days?"

One of her friends nodded and went to Billie's kitchen and retrieved a bottle of vitamin B and several glasses of water.

Sunday morning the persistent ringing of a doorbell awakened Billie. Natalie stood on the doorstep. She took in Billie's swollen squinted eyes and extreme bed-head exacerbated by yesterday's hair gel. "Hey!" Natalie said without preamble. "Why don't you hop in the shower, and we'll go out to breakfast."

Billie attempted a dry gummy reply.

"No. It's nothing fancy. Just a breakfast joint around the corner, really it's been there forever. Get clean. We'll go." And with that, Natalie planted herself on Billie's shabby-chic couch.

Twenty minutes later, in a relic of a coffee shop on a powder blue vinyl banquette, Natalie launched right back into their relationship as if there hadn't been an enormous gap. Natalie dumped a saucer of salsa on her scrambled eggs and said, "You know, everybody does something egregiously stupid when they're young. Probably they engage in a series of egregiously stupid episodes. It's how you learn—stupid to savvy—only now, here, because you married a movie star, you do it in public, with a clamoring audience."

Billie's head throbbed and she wondered why she had missed Natalie's company so much—perhaps, because she was egregiously stupid.

Natalie's advice was always meted out in historical anecdotes. Never a simple, "You fucked up and here's how you fix it," but always with a task of gleaning the message, Natalie began her tale. "You know Pete Fitzgerald?"

A black and white image of a rock-hewn masculine icon standing on the prow of a ship, sword in hand, immediately came to Billie's mind. "Isn't he dead?"

"Sure he's dead. But he was huge. As big a movie career as ever there was."

"Okay." said Billie.

"What you probably don't know is that when he was eighteen, after he was kicked out of Pasadena Junior College…"

"I wasn't kicked out of Harvard."

"Right. After Pete Fitzgerald was kicked out of college, he worked as a male model. That was back in around 1930…Anyway, as you know, he was kinda hot. He caught on with, let's just say, everybody. For a while he was a paid companion, a gigolo. Ladies, gentlemen, you catch my drift?" Billie nodded. She wondered how Natalie seemed to have access to information she'd never heard of, and then she remembered Natalie's father ran a movie studio. For the moment, she glossed over the inference that she was being compared to a teenage gigolo. "Then, one night he gets a gig in downtown L.A., like an appearance, there's a big party, they called it the Sybarite's Ball and it's down at the Biltmore and most of the attendees are men. It's a white-tie-and-tails event and Pete Fitzgerald is there, only he's not wearing anything except some strategically placed fruit, 'cause he's being carried through the tuxedoed crowd on a silver platter in nothing but his beautiful broad shouldered birthday suit. And, somewhere in that crowd, someone realized he had star quality. Everyone says his first movie catapulted him to fame, but really it was that night, the night he was served on a platter."

"Really?" Billie inquired. She was remembering a stellar film career, only interrupted by a stint as a bomber pilot in WWII.

"Really?"

"Really," Natalie said. "Back then, the studios had legions of talent scouts, and once they made their picks, say…at the Sybarite's Ball…press agents constructed and codified personas so thick no trace of scandal ever permeated." Natalie peered expectantly at Billie. Billie wished one of her old friends were there to translate. "Now it's called 'controlling the spin.'"

"Oh. I thought you were trying to tell me, in a nice way, that teenagers are idiots, and that I was, or maybe still am, an idiot." Billie frowned. "And maybe I'm about to get served on a platter. Shit."

"Everybody's an idiot sometime. I'm just suggesting that if you want to come out on top in this situation…"

"In the divorce?"

"In the divorce. If you want to come out on top, you have to learn how to control the spin."

Billie sighed. "Apparently, I don't know how to control anything."

"Look, Toots, this isn't a pity party. Take in the overall picture and then seize your options. There's always a way. You just need to find it."

Two weeks later, after dropping her son off at a preschool from which he would be collected by one of her husband's wenches (a thousand pardons, collected by one of his personal assistants), Billie sat from morning to early evening in an editing bay at USC putting together a three-minute 16mm film. The room was wide open with a wall of north-facing windows. The space featured five twenty-foot-long tables with four editing stations per table. Along the south wall were windowless cubicles that each held a projector and a small screen on a tripod to review works in progress.

Billie liked the regimented room. She liked working with her hands. She liked the process: putting on the thin white disposable cotton gloves so her fingers wouldn't mark the footage, breaking down the raw film reels on a Bell & Howell splicer and hanging it on neat strips on a rack over a bin at her workstation. She liked running the strips back and forth on the illuminated bed until she found where to trim and where to splice. She like the physicality of it, the finality of it, positioning the film sprockets down exactly on the pins, swiping the blade across the film, sanding down the edges of the cut, applying the glue, dropping the plate to make the weld. Repetitive, detailed, and from bits a pieces of celluloid she could make a cohesive narrative. Most of her classes were theoretical, and she found them irritating; there were just so many Jean-Luc Godard films any human being could reasonably stomach. Long lectures on auteur vs. director set her teeth on edge. But editing, structuring, this, she felt, was the real deal. Three minutes of film; it was short, but it was whole, it made sense, and she was in control...control, she really liked being in control.

Suddenly, she felt flushed. For some reason, she remembered the first time she'd had sex with her boyfriend freshman year back in Cambridge and then afterwards hanging out in somebody else's room, crowded with eight of their friends, listening to The Clash, feeling fundamentally changed. She remembered looking around the room in 1979 wondering if anybody else noticed the difference, and for some reason she did the same now, in 1990. She scanned the editing room to see if there was a physical tell for an epiphany moment.

Two young men in their early twenties were hunched down in a darkened cubicle, stubble across their chins, staring at the projection screen. The only thing on their horizon was their unfolding masterpiece. It must have been around five o'clock. The editing room was nearly silent. The population on campus was thinning out in anticipation of altered states and misadventures. At a maternal twenty-nine, Billie felt those days had departed, but something key had suddenly taken their place: she liked control, and she liked the inkling of muscularity, the real labor it took to make even the smallest film.

It was at that moment that Billie pushed aside the strategically placed fruit and came down from her silver platter.

HANK PERRITT

SILVER BULLET

This is a fictional work.
Any resemblance between the characters
and actual persons is purely coincidental.

TIME AND PLACE
Boston 2012

CHARACTERS
Chad Wilbourne, 27-year-old quadriplegic lawyer
Braxton Debardeleben, 23-year-old paralegal

ACT I, SCENE 1

A well-appointed office. Chad is sitting behind the desk. He is a quadriplegic, unable to move his arms, hands, legs, or feet. He can move his head and neck, and his shoulders; that's all. Braxton enters. He is handsome and fit, dressed in a well-tailored suit and tie.

CHAD: You must be the new paralegal.

BRAXTON: I am. Lyman Durstan.

> *[He advances to the desk and extends his hand. Chad's arms and hands do not move.]*

CHAD: Sorry. Consider your hand shaken. They didn't tell you anything about the job requirements.

BRAXTON Oh! I'm terribly sorry! I did know, of course. I hope I haven't embarrassed you.

CHAD: I'm long beyond embarrassment. Sit down.

[Braxton sits and turns chair to face Chad.]

CHAD (cont'd): They told you I need a smart research assistant.

BRAXTON: Yes.

CHAD: One who can put the research results on a screen positioned so I can read it.

BRAXTON: Yes

CHAD: And certain less conventional duties. Sometimes I need something to drink.

BRAXTON: Oh, I don't mind at all—whatever you need.

SCENE 2 (OFFICE, LATER)

BRAXTON: And so this guy, Brendan Scope, and the other student, Bobby Spurlock, just sat there and let the guy drink himself to death?

CHAD: That's what the prosecutor says.

BRAXTON: And it was eight years ago, and they're only now prosecuting him?

CHAD: Do you think the passage of time expunges blame?

BRAXTON: He was a college student then. Now, you say he's a successful and respected young lawyer.

CHAD: Changes according to the rhythms of life. Do you know what a "silver bullet" is?

BRAXTON: I guess it's a bullet made out of silver.

CHAD: The Lone Ranger used silver bullets to signify justice. In folklore, werewolves, witches, and other monsters could be killed only by silver bullets. In software engineering, the phrase signifies a breakthrough that will never happen. It's been my experience that we all seek silver bullets to escape from our pasts, like Brendan or, in some cases, to return to our pasts—like quarterbacking the Notre Dame football team or qualifying for the Navy SEALs. Our client wants a silver bullet to slay his monster. Maybe they'd forget about it with time. That one didn't appear. Maybe they'd give him a break because he was only a college kid then and now the rhythm of life has taken him to a different place. That one didn't appear, either. We're Brendan's last hope for a silver bullet.

[Chad pauses and watches Braxton.]

CHAD (cont'd): Could you get me some coffee? There's a coffee machine in the alcove that brews one cup at a time. Help yourself to one, if you like.

[Braxton goes offstage and returns with two cups of coffee. He sets one by Chad's right hand and sits with his own. Chad looks down. He is unable to do anything with the coffee cup beside his hand.]

CHAD: Could you get me some coffee?

BRAXTON *[confused]:* It's right there. *[horrified]* Oh. I'm sorry. I did it again.

[He stands, hesitates, and then moves slightly behind Chad and lifts the cup to his lips. Chad takes a drink but Braxton does not lower the cup soon enough and Chad chokes. He coughs so vigorously that one of his hands slides backward off the desk and falls.]

BRAXTON: Oh shit! I'm sorry.

[He is not sure what to do. With the sleeve of his suit jacket, he clumsily mops at the coffee on Chad's chin and on the front of his shirt.]

CHAD *[recovering]:* You say that a lot. Now. May I have a cigarette?

BRAXTON: I'm not sure . . .

CHAD: It's a big production to go outside. It's my office. The cigarettes are in my shirt pocket. So's the lighter.

> *[Braxton is uncomfortable with the intimacy represented by reaching into Chad's shirt pocket, but he moves closer, reaching out, and delicately removes the pack of cigarettes and the lighter. Then, he hesitates.]*

BRAXTON: Shall I light it for you, or...?

CHAD: Just put it in my mouth and light it. *[Glances down]* And please put my hand back up on the desk.

> *[Braxton looks in horror at the dangling hand. He can't bring himself to touch it.]*

CHAD (cont'd): You don't have to be afraid of it. It's inert. Braxton complies, and anxiously watches Chad smoke. He occasionally removes the cigarette and then reinserts it between Chad's lips.

CHAD (cont'd): Okay. I'm done.

> *[Braxton removes the cigarette and looks around for a safe place to put the butt. Finally he pinches it out, and drops it into the trashcan.]*

CHAD (cont'd): Rhythms of life.

SCENE 3

CHAD: We all suffer.

BRAXTON: I suppose we do.

CHAD: Why do you suffer?

BRAXTON: I'd just as soon not talk about it.

CHAD: OK. There're some things I don't like to talk about either—actually one main thing.

BRAXTON: How you got hurt.

CHAD: Pretty much.

BRAXTON: How...Oh. I'm sorry. I don't mean to...

[Chad laughs.]

CHAD: Sorry again. Now?

BRAXTON: You said you didn't want to talk about it.

CHAD: No I don't. It's not necessary.

BRAXTON: No, I suppose not.

CHAD: Because you remember.

BRAXTON *[beginning to panic]:* Remember what?

CHAD: How it happened.

BRAXTON: No. I don't know anything about . . .

CHAD: You've come a long way since then. I didn't recognize you, at first. There was a time when everyone said you were stupid, when you were drunk all the time. When you didn't bathe very often.

BRAXTON: You must have me confused with someone else.

CHAD: And then someone took you under his wing. You couldn't understand why he would. No one else ever had—well, a couple of times people seemed to, but they just did it because they wanted something from you, or because they wanted to belittle you.

BRAXTON: I don't want to talk about the past.

CHAD: I expect not. And this guy who took you under his wing coaxed you into running, exercising, getting into some kind of physical shape. He encouraged you, never made fun of you. Had adult conversations with you. Respected you.

BRAXTON: I admired him. I worshiped him.

CHAD: Maybe even loved him a little. And apparently he got something started because you are not back there anymore.

BRAXTON: No.

CHAD: You are here.

BRAXTON: Yes.

CHAD: But you remember sometimes.

[Braxton is in a trance, unable to say anything]

CHAD (cont'd): You remember how hot it was, how, when you walked, the sandy ground swallowed your boots. The little clearing where pine trees hadn't been planted yet. The pickup truck parked in the clearing. How you set up the targets and were practicing shooting. And, then, how one of your buddies shot a drugged dart and hit someone in his bare shoulder. And how the three of you then spread-eagled him across the edge of the truck bed.

BRAXTON *[dreamily]*: And then took a sledgehammer...

CHAD: And swung it as hard as you could.

BRAXTON: And hit him squarely on the back of the neck.

CHAD: You were eager to go first. You wanted to do it again, harder.

[Braxton looks at him and breaks into uncontrollable sobs.]

CHAD (CONT'D): And so here we are. There is no silver bullet. Not for me. Not for you. I would be interested to know, however:

BRAXTON *[looking up through tears]*: Why I did it?

CHAD: No. That's immaterial. Knowing why is not a silver bullet.

BRAXTON: What, then?

CHAD: Why you're here now.

MELANIE VILLINES

SILVER BELLS, SILVER BELLS

Vance Middlebrooks had no idea what kind of writing services he was supposed to provide at the gig he'd found on Craigslist. But *silver bells, silver bells* it was Christmastime in the city—and he needed cash. He'd do just about anything, writing-wise, for a few extra bucks.

When Vance showed up at the appointed address on a Hollywood side street, he was surprised to find Griffin Gnowles, the red carpet interviewer, there to greet him—mannered, manicured, and manscaped to perfection.

After the introductions, Vance said: "So, what are we doing today?"

Griffin pretended not to hear the question and headed up the stairs to a small yellow brick house that looked as if it could have belonged to Little Pig number three.

As they waited for someone to open the door, Vance noticed that every two seconds Griffin checked his watch, a Rolex. Vance made a mental note to add this to the file of quirks, flaws, and tics he kept at home.

When developing characters for his screenplays, Vance pulled various traits from the list and combined them into—voila!—a person. There was a certain godlike thrill to breathing life into these characters—how they looked, who they were, their names, traits, habits, and all the rest.

Griffin banged on the door with this fist. "We're here," he said. "Open up."

Again, the celebrity interviewer checked his Rolex, a watch that Vance knew was worth more than many cars—including his own 1998 Toyota Corolla, which he tried to avoid being seen in. Vance usually left his vehicle far from his destination, which is what he'd done today. He'd arrived early, parked four blocks away, and walked in the Yuletide cold to the meeting place.

When the door swung open, a tall, heavyset, middle-aged man stood there. He was dressed in a red-and-black-checked flannel shirt and black pants with red suspenders.

"Hello! Hello!" the man bellowed. "Glad you're here," he said, then stepped aside as Griffin and Vance entered.

After they walked through the door, the man kicked it closed with his foot. Vance noticed he was wearing Timberland boots. The boots looked new and so did the man's clothes, as if he'd just obtained them from a studio costume department.

"Dr. Bing, this is our writer," Griffin said. "The one whose résumé we discussed."

"Maxwell!" Bing boomed, while clapping Vance on the back.

When Vance opened his mouth to correct Dr. Bing, he felt Griffin's elbow in his side.

"Maxwell comes highly recommended," Griffin said.

"Of course. Of course," Dr. Bing roared, again giving Vance a few raps on the back. "We're so happy you're with us, Maxwell."

As Vance looked up at Dr. Bing—the man was 6'4" to his 5'10"—he wondered what "with us" meant. Who was "us," and what did it mean to be "with" them? And, most of all, he wondered why they were calling him Maxwell.

"Glad to be here," Vance responded and looked to Griffin, hoping he'd fill in some details.

"Is everyone here?" Griffin asked.

"Everybody's ready," Bing replied.

Vance wondered who "everybody" was and what "ready" meant. Simple words had taken on mystery and significance. He was a writer, yet the most basic words were stumping him.

"That's good," Vance said, just to join into the conversation. He had no idea whether it was good or not.

"I detect a note of impatience in your voice," Bing said, focusing a gray stare at Vance.

"Not at all," Vance answered, feeling his face flush. "If anything, I'm just eager to learn more about the project."

"Hasn't Griffin told you?"

Griffin glared at him, making it clear that he wasn't about to jump in and save the moment.

"I'd like to hear about it from you, Dr. Bing," Vance said.

"From your résumé, I understand you're an award-winning medical writer with a specialty in mental illness and schizophrenia," Bing said, his eyes cold and stony.

Vance looked to Griffin, who widened his eyes—meaning, "don't blow this."

"Of course," Vance replied. The closest he'd come to medical writing was a cheap-o script he'd drafted about a zombie leprosy outbreak.

"Let's get started, then," Bing said, extending his hand in a "this way" gesture. "The facility is out back. We have twenty-eight residents."

Dr. Bing pushed open some French doors, and about fifty feet away Vance saw a beige stucco building that looked as if it had once been a Mexican restaurant. One of Vance's hobbies was photographing repurposed buildings—and there were many in Los Angeles, the megapolis that was always busy turning into something else.

Vance turned to say something to Griffin and was shocked to find him gone. All that lay behind him was the yellow brick house he'd just exited and a burnt-toast-looking patch of grass that he'd just walked upon.

Dr. Bing called out, "Come along, Maxwell."

"Where's Griffin?" Vance asked Dr. Bing as he approached the front door.

"He's with the crew," Bing responded, then placed his meatloaf-sized hand on the black iron handle and started to push the door open.

Vance wondered who the "crew" was? A film crew? Some of the facility's twenty-eight residents?

"Oh, the crew," Vance replied, then heard his stomach growl in a loud, pleading roar.

"Hungry? Or are you nervous?" Bing asked.

Vance figured Dr. Bing was a psychiatrist or psychoanalyst—and, like most people in his line of work, analyzed the behavior and attitudes of everyone around him. At least this was what Vance figured psychiatrists and their ilk were like—he'd included "makes snap judgments" on his list of tics, quirks, and traits related to mental health professionals.

"It must be close to lunchtime," Vance replied.

"Depends on what time you have lunch," Bing said.

Vance stepped into the building's vestibule and took a quick look around. The place was pretty much as he'd expected. It looked like the waiting area of a typical Mexican restaurant—stucco walls, wrought iron and glass light fixtures hanging from the ceiling, terra cotta tiles on the floor. There were also winding staircases on both the left and right.

Dr. Bing closed the door and stood next to Vance. He checked his watch.

"Two minutes early," Bing said. "But I'd rather be early than late." He snapped his suspenders and turned to Vance. "How about you, Maxwell?"

"Depends on whether I'm going to the dentist or the movies," Vance replied, figuring Dr. Bing might smile or even chuckle.

But chuckling seemed to be the last thing on Dr. Bing's mind. His eyes formed into gray slits that seemed to be the entrance to an unremitting void.

"Are you aware, Maxwell, that you use techniques of avoidance to evade direct responses to simple questions? Were you the youngest child in your family?"

"Actually, I was the oldest," Vance replied.

"Well, sometimes the oldest tries to gain attention by giving flip answers."

"Is the two minutes up?" Vance said.

"The two-minute warning. Is that what you mean?" Dr. Bing asked, scratching his bristly gray and white beard.

"I was just trying to make conversation," Vance responded.

"Well, if you're trying to make conversation, say something that the other party would find interesting."

Vance wanted to ask whether analysts were exempt from common courtesy and could express themselves with impunity in the rudest possible terms, but he had come this far.

"Excellent point," Vance said, shifting from foot to foot. He needed to use a restroom and glanced around for a sign or a marked door.

"Looking for a washroom?" Dr. Bing asked.

"Yes," Vance said.

When Dr. Bing didn't respond, Vance asked: "Where can I find one?"

"At the top of the stairs on your left," Bing said, then added: "I wish you wouldn't have waited so long to say something. Hurry or you're going to get us off schedule."

Vance wanted to ask, "Off schedule for fricking what???" but merely smiled, nodded, and bolted up the stairway, taking the steps two at a time.

Vance entered the restroom, rushed into the stall, and locked the door behind him. But as soon as he was poised to do what he'd come to do, he couldn't do it. If he'd been at home, he would have run the water in the basin. But the basins were on the other side of the room. God, what a dilemma. He closed his eyes and tried to think of a flowing garden hose and water running into a bathtub.

"Hurry up!" Dr. Bing yelled through the door. "We're going to be late."

Ahh. Flow at last.

Vance heard the door open and then the sound of footsteps.

"You in here, Maxwell?" Bing said.

"Just a sec," Vance responded. He couldn't believe anyone would be rude enough to hurry a grown man out of a toilet. For God's sake, I could be really sick. Why does he assume I'm dawdling and need to be hurried along?

"Make it snappy," Bing said.

Vance heard the door open and close.

As he was finishing what he'd started, Vance had an insight about his screenplay. He realized how to solve a longstanding problem. All at once, the ideas gushed into his brain. He pulled a notebook and pen from the pocket of his parka and began to jot down the notes as fast as he could. He propped the notebook against the wall of the stall and wrote with his Bic pen. But after a few words, the Bic went dry, so he stopped and shook it, then propped the notebook on his knee and began to write again.

God, God, oh God, Vance thought, why couldn't I have been at home when this gusher blew? He tried to write as fast as he could, crouched down in the toilet stall with the notebook on his knee and the black ink trailing across the paper. He tried to think of a form of shorthand that he'd remember when he got home. The words were just coming so fast that it was as if they had completely bypassed his brain and were communicating directly with his right hand. After a minute of this, Vance no longer even tried to follow the trajectory of the words or what they meant. He was just a vehicle that the story was passing through and he was trying his best to get it all down.

Bang, bang, bang.

"Maxwell! What's in the name of God is taking so long?" Bing yelled through the door.

"Be right out," Vance yelled back, as his hand raced across the notebook page.

He wasn't sure what he was writing, but it seemed as if he had finally figured out how the dystopian world in his screenplay fit together. He had a sense, too, that he had solved the most difficult problem with the script—the ending. But it was coming too fast for Vance to even get an inkling of what it was all about. He just prayed he could read his handwriting when he got home.

Bang, bang, bang.

"How much longer?" Bing asked, incredulous.

"I think I have food poisoning," Vance shouted over the top of the stall.

"Good God!"

Vance continued to glide his pen across the paper—feeling elated, almost as if he were a maestro conducting an orchestra. Yes, his Bic was his baton and it was flowing, flowing, flowing with beautiful words. He was sure they were beautiful. They had to be. The story was writing itself—every writer's dream, and it was happening to him: Vance Middlebrooks.

"Maxwell, what the hell's going on?"

It was Griffin. Vance wondered where he'd been since he'd disappeared outside.

"Food poisoning," Vance said and continued to write.

He looked down and saw Griffin's shiny five-hundred-dollar Ferragamo pumps right outside the stall. A second later, he was looking into Griffin's face as he bent down to glare at him from under the stall's door. Griffin's eyes darted from Vance's face to his notebook and pen.

"You're in there *writing*?" Griffin said, his voice rising to nearly a shriek. He spit out the word "writing" as if it were a felony offense.

Vance stared from his writing trance into Griffin's face, which was puffed up with anger and dotted with purple blotches that looked like thunderclouds.

"I'm making a few notes," Vance said, continuing to write, as if his hand were a separate entity with its own will and consciousness.

"Come out of there immediately!" Griffin commanded.

When Vance didn't respond, Griffin grabbed the top of the stall's door and began to shake it, then press against it with his full weight. Somehow the door held, leaving Vance a private cubicle in which to continue to commit words to paper.

"What the hell's the matter with you?" Griffin screeched.

Griffin kept shaking the door and pressing on it, but the sturdy slide-latch lock and metal door held fast. The next thing he realized, Griffin was walking toward the restroom exit. Vance heard the door open and close and then the only sound was the plop, plop, plop of water in one of the basins.

"Tad-da!" his pen seemed to say as it stabbed Vance's notebook with a final period.

Now, the next best thing to a gusher—reading what he'd written while under the spell. He intended to sit on the floor of the stall and pore over the words. This was always so surprising and amazing to Vance. Most of the time, he had little recollection of what he'd actually put on paper. He was reading the words as if for the first time—and what he found there was always a revelation. He saw the intelligent design at work, saw how some part of his mind—his subconscious, his unconscious, his psyche—had had figured it all out.

Vance took a deep breath. He flipped up the hood on his parka and leaned his head against the wall of the toilet stall. He held the notebook to his chest with his left hand and with his right hand clutched his trusty Bic pen. He kept his eyes closed and savored the moment, forgetting for a few seconds where he was and the fact that he had just defied two by-now irate clients.

He felt euphoric—it was a feeling of relief and peace and completion and happiness. Merry Christmas. All was right with the world.

BARBARA EKNOIAN

GLIMMER

Sun filters through the white
curtains over my kitchen sink
on to the breakfast table.
I'm relieved to be home
safe from our trip.
It is a perfect sunny day
but I'm worrying about health
concerns for our family.

I rise from the chair puzzled
when the room darkens.
What happened
to the sunshine?
I look out the window toward
the eastern blue sky where
white energetic clouds dance.
But right above my house
a huge charcoal gray cloud
blankets the white cloud
whose edges peek out
from under
forming a glittering outline
around the dark gray mass.

I load the dishwasher,
sweep the floor, then notice
sunshine that spills
through the window again.
I smile because I just saw
a cloud with a silver lining.

RUTH MOON KEMPHER

CONJURE, WITH CURE

Mis Tijeras—

my scissors
sat on the table
rusted in the crotch &
wouldn't cut butter
without a jag
but
gypsy lady
whispered them silver
sharp enough to cut stars
& houses & trees of glass—
the catch, of course
they stuck to the hand
of anyone who used them. Long
after the cutting, they burned
finger loops into skin.
Only silver
of course
would lift the curse.

JANE BUEL BRADLEY

A SILVER EYELASH

A silver eyelash in the sunset sky

draws me outside to look and dream the why

this monthly promise always stirs my soul

and keeps me hopeful that before the whole

full moon lights up the autumn's darkest night

I shall find words to speak of my delight

in this world's beauty and begin to face

the waning and the darkness with some grace

(with thanks to Robert Frost's "Moon Compasses")

JOAN JOBE SMITH

ENDLESS RIVER OF SILVERY MOONS

Everything was silver when I was a kid with
Hi Ho Silver! and Lone Ranger silver bullets
as silver airplanes flew off to World War 2,
all of our money silver dimes and dollars,
movie stars on the big silver screen smiling
silver teeth wore silver streaked hair, drove cars
made of silver-hump bumpers, big-grinning grills
and hubcaps silver glitter swirls beneath silvery fog
sunsets in San Francisco while I set the supper table
with silver forks, spoons and knives and sometimes
after they tucked me into bed my mother and father
in the living room cheek to cheek danced in the dark
while Artie Shaw's 78 clarinet played "Stardust"
and I watched, waited to grow up to live my life, too,
beside the light of an endless river of silvery moons.

ABOUT THE AUTHORS

BARBARA ALFARO is a graduate of Goddard College and the American Academy of Dramatic Arts. She is the recipient of a Maryland State Arts Council Individual Artist Award for her play *Dos Madres*. Her poems and essays have appeared in various literary journals. The paperback edition of her poems called *Singing Magic* and the Kindle edition of her poetry titled *First Kiss* are available on Amazon. *Mirror Talk,* her memoir about a Catholic girlhood and working in theatre won the 2012 IndieReader Discovery Award for Best Memoir and is also available on Amazon. Visit Barbara's website at www.BarbaraAlfaro.net

JENA ARDELL is a freelance photographer and writer. Her photography has been exhibited worldwide and has appeared in numerous publications, including *Rolling Stone*, and can be found as the cover art to a handful of novels. She is a regular contributing writer and concert photographer for *L.A. Weekly's* music and arts sections. Jena earned second place in the online feature category at the L.A. Press Club's National Entertainment Journalism Awards 2011 for her contribution to *L.A. Weekly's* Coachella coverage. Jena is currently pursuing editorial photography and seeking a publisher for a children's book she penned during a cross-country train trip.

MELISSA BERRY is a third generation Los Angelino with a BA from Immaculate Heart College in English and Theatre, and minors in Music, Art, and History, and recent MA in Humanities from Mount St. Mary's College. While living in downtown Los Angeles, she currently writes for numerous publications, including Examiner.com and *Smooth Jazz*. Over fifty-four of her articles are available at Buzzine.com. She is also a published author and English instructor. Visit her at www.melissamillerberry.org.

JANE BUEL BRADLEY's first book, *World Alive,* appeared from PEARL Editions when she was eighty-nine years old, and was followed two years later by *Tree of Life*. Jane continued to write poetry until shortly before her death two months shy of her ninety-fourth birthday. Jane was a beloved children's librarian in Long Beach, California, a political and environmental activist, and an inspiration to all who knew her. She was the niece of Ernest Thayer, author of the beloved classic baseball poem "Casey at the Bat."

JOHN BRANTINGHAM's poetry and fiction have been published in hundreds of magazines and venues, including Garrison Keillor's *Writer's Almanac, PEARL, Tears in the Fence, Confrontation,* and *The Journal.* His books include *East of Los Angeles* and *Let Us All Pray to Our Own Strange Gods* (forthcoming from World Parade Books). He works at Mt. San Antonio College, where he teaches English and directs the creative writing programs.

RACHEL CAREY is a writer and filmmaker. She received an MFA in Film Directing from NYU, an M.Ed. from Harvard, and a BA in English from Yale. She currently lives with her family in New Jersey and teaches college film classes. Silver Birch Press will publish her debut novel, *Debt,* in 2013.

CHIWAN CHOI is a writer, editor, teacher, and co-founder of Writ Large Press. His poems and essays have appeared in numerous journals and magazines, including *ONTHEBUS,* Esquire.com, and *The Nervous Breakdown.* His first major collection of poetry, *The Flood,* was published by Tía Chucha Press in April 2010. His second collection, *Abductions,* was published by Writ Large Press in April 2012.

BILLY COOK lives and writes in San Francisco, although you may have encountered silverware with which he has eaten in Chicago, New York, or Michigan.

BARBARA DAHL is the pen name of a Midwestern author.

WALTER DE LA MARE (1873-1956) was an English poet, short story writer, and novelist. His 1921 novel *Memoirs of a Midget* won the James Tait Black Memorial Prize for fiction and his *Collected Stories for Children* won the 1947 Carnegie Medal for British children's books.

COLLEEN DELEGAN, a writer and producer, lives in Chicago. She spent five years in Europe and Asia, collecting material and traveling extensively. She has written pilots for NBC, CBS, and ABC in addition to several screenplays. In a previous life, Colleen was president of her own advertising agency, "Delegan & Kimmel, Words & Pictures," and was a creative director for Leo Burnett, U.S.A. Her first book, *Three Thousand Coffees in Vienna,* was published in 2004. She is currently under contract to ghostwrite a murder mystery.

GILLIAN EATON teaches in the School of Music Theater and Dance at the University of Michigan, Ann Arbor. She is an award-winning director, actress, and educator. In 2012, she completed an MA in Creative Writing at the University of Wales, Trinity St. David, gaining a first with distinction. Her work has been published in the *Lampeter Review, Hungry Hill Writers Journal,* and in various anthologies. She won the Poetry meets Politics Prize in Ireland and was honored by PEN in Los Angeles for poetry about L.A.

BARBARA EKNOIAN's work has appeared in *PEARL, Chiron Review, Re)verb,* and *Cradle Song,* a motherhood anthology. She has received two Pushcart Prize nominations, and is a member of Donna Hilbert's poetry workshop in Long Beach, California. Her fiction was featured in the 2009 Sixth Annual Emerging Voices Show produced by Sally Shore's New Short Fiction Series. She hails from New Jersey and has never lost her accent.

MERRILL FARNSWORTH is a Nashville-based writer, artist, and therapist. Born among the Texas tumbleweeds, Merrill came of age reveling in the sights and sounds of Puerto Rico's Afro-Caribbean culture. The cadences of South Carolina left their mark on her, as did melodies reaching from Appalachia to the Mississippi Delta. She is a published poet and award-winning lyricist, and recently collaborated with Phil Madeira on the Americana release *Mercyland*. In 2012, Silver Birch Press published *Jezebel's Got the Blues...And Other Works of Imagination*, Merrill's collection of performance pieces that was selected for 2012's The Puzzle, a festival of plays held in New York City. For more about Merrill, visit www.writingcircle.org.

SYED AFZAL HAIDER is a writer and founding editor of *Chicago Quarterly Review*. His short stories and essays have appeared in a variety of literary magazines including *Saint Ann's Review, AmerAsia, Rambunctious Review, The Journal of Pakistani Literature, The Taylor Trust, Trajectory, Marco Polo*. Indian Voices, Oxford University Press, Milkweed Editions, Penguin Books, and Longman Literature have anthologized Haider. His short story collection, *Tumbleweed Connection*, was a finalist for the 2004 MVP competition. His first novel, *To Be With Her*, was published in 2010, and his second novel, *Life of Ganesh*, is forthcoming. He lives in Evanston, Illinois, with his wife and is father of two wonderful grown-up sons. He can be reached by email at sahaider@sbcglobal.net.

JOE HAKIM is a writer, poet, and spoken-word performer from Hull, East Yorkshire, U.K. He has performed at many venues and events around Britain, including Latitude Festival, Big Chill Festival, and the Edinburgh Fringe Festival. He is the co-organizer and host of "Write to Speak," a series of spoken-word events held at Hull Truck Theatre. His debut book, *No Light/Might Escape,* was published by Night Publishing. He recently wrote and directed his first play, *Blackout,* which was performed in September 2012 at Hull Truck Theatre as part of Greyscale Theatre's *Theatre Brothel 2.0.*

ANDREW HILBERT lives and works in Austin, Texas. His poetry has been published in numerous magazines and websites, including *Chiron Review, PEARL, Out of the Gutter*, and *Nerve Cowboy.* On his blog, cheesepaper.blogspot.com, his chapbook, *At the Thrift Store,* can be purchased.

DONNA HILBERT's latest book, *The Green Season,* World Parade Books, a collection of poems, stories, and essays, is now available in an expanded second edition. Donna appears in and her poetry is the text of the documentary *Grief Becomes Me: A Love Story*, a Christine Fugate film. Earlier books include *Mansions* and *Deep Red* from Event Horizon, *Transforming Matter* and *Traveler in Paradise* from PEARL Editions, and the short story collection *Women Who Make Money and the Men Who Love Them* from Staple First Editions (published in England). Poems in Italian can be found in Bloc notes 59 and in French in *La page blanche*, in both cases translated by Mariacristina Natalia Bertoli. New work is in recent or forthcoming issues of *5AM, Nerve Cowboy, PEARL,* and *Poets & Artists.* A new collection, *The Congress of Luminous Bodies,* is forthcoming from Aortic Books. Learn more at www.donnahilbert.com.

GAIA HOLMES lives in Halifax, United Kingdom. She is a part-time creative writing lecturer at the University of Huddersfield and freelance writer who works with schools, libraries, and other community groups throughout the West Yorkshire region. In her spare time, Gaia is a DJ for Phoenix FM, the Borough of Calderdale's community radio station. She also bangs and rattles a red tambourine at gigs and rehearsals with Sambalifax and squeezes an accordion with Crow Hill Stompers. Her second poetry collection, *Lifting the Piano with One Hand,* was published in 2012 by Comma Press.

ZACK HUNTER is a synesthetic insomniac who loves nothing more than to explore the mysterious nature of our being. He was born in California after being implanted in a laboratory and has been writing ever since his first puff of cannabis at thirteen.

DIANE EAGLE KATAOKA lives at eight thousand feet in the Eastern Sierra, where she skis and hikes. A researcher for the late Leon Uris *(Trinity* and *The Haj),* she was director of marketing and communications for the Music Academy of the West, as well as editor-in-chief of the *Mammoth Times* and *Mammoth Sierra Magazine.* She is currently a freelance writer and editor, poet and blogger. (Visit her blog at mammothlakesview.com.) Her chapbook *Snow Globe,* published by Two Birds Press, is a poetic history of five seasons in a mountain ski town.

RUTH MOON KEMPHER, an ex-navy brat who was born in Red Bank, New Jersey, has had her poetry and short prose appear in journals and other periodical publications since 1958, and has published many other people's work since 1994 through her Kings Estate Press in St. Augustine, Florida. She is retired from owning a tavern and from teaching—first for Flagler College while attaining her BA and graduating with the college's first class; and later, after achieving her MA at Emory University in Atlanta, in the English Department of St. Johns River Community College. The latest of her thirty-three (mostly small) collections of verse will also include prose pieces—*Key West Papers* is due from Casa de Cinco Hermanos Press, Pueblo, Colorado, in late 2012 or early 2013. After years of living at the beach, she now lives in the woods in an old cracker house with two dogs, Sadie, a long-legged hound, and Mister Frost, an emotional American Husky.

LINDA KING is a poet, playwright, and artist working in painting and sculpture who was immortalized in the poetry and prose of her former love Charles Bukowski. During the 1970s, King edited the little magazine *Purr.* She also has had her poetry published in a wide variety of magazines, including *The Bukowski Review* and *Wormwood Review.* Her most recent works are the memoir *Loving and Hating Bukowski* and the novel *Mad Ouija.*

THOMAS KUDLA is a graduate of Indiana University, Bloomington. With the help of his tailored degree from the Individualized Major Program at IUB and a grant from the Indiana University

Hutton Honors College, he was able to write his first novel, *Confessions of an American*. His book *What My Brain Told Me* was selected as a finalist in the short story nonfiction category of the 2009 National Indie Excellence Awards. For two years, Thom was an editor with the Sun-Times News Group. In 2011, he founded To a T Editorial Group, a manuscript editing business. To learn more about Thom, visit thomkudla.com.

MORIAH LACHAPELL was born in Oregon and earned her bachelor's degree from Western Oregon University. She also studied Viticulture at Washington State University and currently works in horticulture. She lives in McMinnville, Oregon, with her daughter and husband.

LEEANNE MCILROY LANGTON is a Senior English Language Fellow for The U.S. Department of State and Georgetown University as well as a lecturer at California State University, Long Beach. A native Californian, she earned a BA in Linguistics from UCLA. and an MA in Linguistics from CSULB. In 2011, she was named "Most Valuable Professor" by the Honors Program at CSULB, where she also works as a faculty mentor for first-generation college students. She is the mother of two daughters.

VICKIE LESTER's people came from Moscow and a London slum called Whitechapel. When the British portion of the family arrived in New York, they headed out to Seattle by train, way before the plane was invented. Finding only rain and more rain, mud, and wooden planks for sidewalks (a segment of which appeared to be an orange crate from sunny California), they immediately booked tickets south...Or so the story goes. And, thus, her father's grandparents came to L.A. Her friends and family continue to toil in the industry, and she tells her tales of beguiling Hollywood under the name Vickie Lester.

ELLARAINE LOCKIE is a widely published and awarded poet, nonfiction book author, and essayist. Her ninth and recent chapbook, *Wild as in Familiar,* was a finalist in the Finishing Line Press Chapbook contest and received *The Aurorean's* Chapbook Pick for Spring 2012. Ellaraine teaches poetry workshops and serves as poetry editor for the lifestyles magazine, *Lilipoh,* and as associate editor for *Mobius*. Silver Birch Press will publish her chapbook *Coffee House Confessions* in 2013.

GERALD LOCKLIN is a professor emeritus of English at California State University, Long Beach, where he taught full-time from 1965-2007, retains his office and contact information, and still teaches an occasional class as needed. He has published fiction, poetry, essays, and reviews prolifically in periodicals and in over a hundred and fifty books, chapbooks, and broadsides. Recent or upcoming books include a fiction e-Book, *The Sun Also Rises in the Desert,* from Mendicant Bookworks, a collection of poems from 2008-present from PRESA Press, three simultaneously released novellas from Spout Press, a new edition of *Gerald Locklin: New and Selected Poems* from Silver Birch Press (formerly from World Parade Books), and a French collection of his prose, *Candy Bars: Le Dernier des Damnes,* due May 7, 2013, from 13e Note Press, Paris. Event Horizon Press released new editions of *A Simpler Time, A Simpler Place* and *Hemingway Colloquium: The Poet Goes to Cuba* in 2011; Coagula Press released the first of two volumes of his *Complete Coagula Poems;* and *From a Male Perspective* appeared from PRESA Press. Contact Gerald Locklin by email at gerlocklin@gmail.com, on Facebook at www.facebook.com/geraldlocklin, and at www.geraldlocklin.org.

AMY LOWELL (1874-1925) was an American poet of the imagist school from Brookline, Massachusetts, who posthumously won the Pulitzer Prize for Poetry in 1926.

SANDYLEE MACCOBY has been a successful portrait painter and teacher of French and Spanish. As a child, she was a competitive figure skater and trained with world-renowned Gus Lussi. She retired from the sport at age thirteen. A graduate of Smith College, she is married to Michael Maccoby, PhD, a psychoanalyst and author, and lives in Washington, D.C.

TAMARA MADISON teaches English and French at a public high school in Los Angeles. Raised on a citrus farm in the California desert, Tamara's life has taken her many places, including Europe and the former Soviet Union, where she spent fifteen months in the 1970s. A swimmer and dog lover, Tamara says, "All I ever wanted to do with my life was write, and I mostly write poetry because it suits my lifestyle; I like the way one can say so much in the economical space of a poem."

CLINT MARGRAVE lives in Long Beach, California. His first full-length collection of poems, *The Early Death of Men,* is newly released from NYQ Books. His work has also appeared or is forth-coming in *The New York Quarterly, Rattle, Ambit* (UK), *3AM* (UK), *PEARL, Serving House Journal, Word Riot,* and *Nerve Cowboy,* among others.

DANIEL MCGINN's work has appeared in the *OC Weekly, Next Magazine,* and other publications. His full-length collection of poems, *1000 Black Umbrellas,* is available from Write Bloody Press. He is currently a student in the low-residency MFA program at Vermont College of Fine Arts. He and his wife are natives of Southern California. They have three children, five grandchildren, and a very good dog.

MARCIA MEARA is a native Floridian living in the Orlando area with her husband of twenty-six years, two silly little dachshunds, and four big, lazy cats. She's fond of reading, gardening, hiking, ca-noeing, painting, and writing, not necessarily in that order. But her favorite thing in the world is spending time with her seven-year-old granddaughter, the world's funniest little girl. She and her husband are looking forward to the birth of their second grandchild in April 2013. Marcia is currently working on her first book, a romantic thriller set in the Blue Ridge Mountains, which she hopes will prove that it's never too late to follow your dream.

ANN MENEBROKER lives in Sacramento, California, and has been writing and publishing since the late 1950s. A long-time member of the Sacramento Poetry Center, she has published over twenty books and chapbooks, has her work on broadsides, been in anthologies, edited literary publications, taught in pris-ons, and has her poems in a college textbook, *Literature and Its Writers.* Her last publication is *The Measure of Small Gratitudes,* 2011, from Kamini Press, Sweden.

JACK MICHELINE was born in the East Bronx, New York, on November 6, 1929, as Harold Martin Silver. Informally educated, he identified closely with the traditions of American vagabond poets, such as Vachel Lindsay and Maxwell Bodenheim, and moved to Greenwich Village in the 1950s to find an outlet for his poetry. In 1958, Troubadour Press published his book, *River of Red Wine,* which was reviewed by Dorothy Parker in *Esquire.* Even though he pro-claimed himself unaffiliated with any group, Micheline appeared fre-quently at poetry readings with Beat writers. He passed away in 1998.

BEN MYERS was born in Durham, United Kingdom, in 1976. His novels include *Pig Iron* (Bluemoose Books) and *Richard* (Picador). His stories, poems, articles, and interviews have appeared in numerous magazines, newspapers, and anthologies. He lives in Mytholmroyd, West Yorkshire, United Kingdom. Find him online at www.benymersmanofletters.blogspot.com.

JAX NTP is a graduate student at Cal State Long Beach in the Masters of Fine Arts, Creative Writing Program. Her poetry has been featured on KBeach Radio, *Moon Tide Press*, *Subliminal Interiors*, and *The Más Tequila Review*. She is editor-in-chief of CSULB's Literary Journal, *RipRap* Volume 35. "Medusa Sonata" won The Aquarium of the Pacific's 3rd Annual Urban Ocean Poetry Festival in May 2012.

HANK PERRITT is the author of four full-length plays, *You Took Away My Flag: a Musical About Kosovo*, *Giving Ground*, *Airline Miles*, and *Goal to Go*; four novels, *Arian*, *Jovan*, *Laser and the Stork*, and *Chad and the Seals*; a movie screenplay based on the story in the musical; and several short plays and movies. He is a law professor in Chicago, where he also serves on the board of The Artistic Home Theatre Company, produces plays and movies, and encourages indie artists.

MEGHAN PINSON lives in Los Angeles with her brilliant sons and a friendly cat. She launched My Two Cents Editing in 2009 and has been happy ever since. Find her at mytwocentsediting.com.

JACKIE PLEDGER-SKWERSKI, following a fifty-year career in business and newspaper journalism, has turned to her true love, fiction. Her feature stories have been published in newspapers and her short stories have appeared in anthologies. She holds a bachelor's degree in education from Purdue University and a master's degree in journalism from Indiana University. She also has taught journalism at Triton Community College and Wilbur Wright College.

KATHY DAHMS ROGERS was born in Iowa, lives in Long Beach, California, and loves to travel with her husband Jack. She calls herself an "accidental poet" because she began writing poetry during the 1990s in a workshop she thought was going to focus on memoir and travel writing. She continues to attend these weekly workshops with poet Donna Hilbert. Now a retired college reading instructor, Kathy's poems have been published in *PEARL*, a literary journal, and *Voices*, an anthology.

CONRAD ROMO grew up on the other side of the tracks in L.A., short, stocky, and swarthy. He is the producer and host of one of the very best literary reading events in L.A.—Tongue & Groove at the Hotel Café, now in its ninth year. Each month, he blends a handpicked mix of writers to present short fiction, poetry, personal essays, along with a musical guest. His writing has appeared in *Los Angeles Review, Wednesday Magazine, Noveltown, Tu Ciudad, Brooklyn & Boyle, Palehouse, Huizache,* and *Latinos in Lotusland.* Visit Conrad at the Tongue & Groove website: tongueandgroovela.com.

LUKE SALAZAR—Thwarting Your Efforts Since 1972. Luke has worked as a repoman, database guru, forklift driver, and licensed private investigator…but never all at once. He holds an MFA in Creative Writing from California State University, Long Beach, and currently works as an editor at a newswire—sprinkling hyphens and commas into poorly written corporate press releases. Luke's poetry can be found in publications such as *PEARL, Ambit* (UK), *The Ledge, Chiron Review, Re)verb, Spot Lit Magazine, MEAT Magazine* (UK), and more. In October 2012, Aortic Press published *California Burning,* Luke's first full-length collection of poetry. For a cranial field trip, visit lukesalazar.com. Luke's contribution to the Silver Anthology first appeared in *Spot Literary Magazine.*

JOAN JOBE SMITH, founding editor of *PEARL* and *Bukowski Review,* worked for seven years as a go-go dancer before receiving her BA from CSULB and MFA from University of California, Irvine. A Pushcart Honoree, her award-winning work has appeared internationally in more than five hundred publications, including *Outlaw Bible, Ambit, Beat Scene, Wormwood Review,* and *Nerve Cowboy*—and she has published twenty collections, including *Jehovah Jukebox* (Event Horizon Press, US) and *The Pow Wow Cafe* (The Poetry Business, UK), a finalist for the UK 1999 Forward Prize. In July 2012, with her husband, poet Fred Voss, she did her sixth reading tour of England (debuting at the 1991 Aldeburgh Poetry Festival), featured at the Humber Mouth Literature Festival in Hull. In November 2012, Silver Birch Press published her literary profile entitled *Charles Bukowski Epic Glottis: His Art & His Women (& me).* In 2013, World Parade Books will release her memoir *Tales of an Ancient Go-Go Girl.* Her literary magazine *PEARL* will release its 50th edition in 2013—find out more at pearlmag.com.

CLIFTON SNIDER, faculty emeritus at Cal State University, Long Beach, is the internationally acclaimed, award-winning author of ten books of poetry, including his latest, *Moonman: New and Selected Poems*, published by World Parade Books in spring 2012. His novel about a bisexual 1980s New Wave rock star, *Loud Whisper* (2000), has been optioned by the independent film company Iconoclastic Features. His coming out/coming of age novel, *Bare Roots*, was published in 2001, as was his novel about two gay sons of a Pentecostal preacher, *Wrestling with Angels: A Tale of Two Brothers*. A Jungian/Queer literary critic, his book, *The Stuff That Dreams Are Made On: A Jungian Interpretation of Literature*, was published in 1991, and he has published hundreds of poems, fiction, and articles internationally, and at CSULB has taught seminars on Virginia Woolf, the Brontë Sisters, Emily Dickinson, and Oscar Wilde. His work has been translated into French and Russian.

DALE SPROWL teaches writing at Biola University in La Mirada, California. During summers, she administrates and teaches at the Young Writer's Project at UCI. Her work with the UCI Writing Project began in 1981, and she has contributed to the UCIWP texts on the teaching of writing. Her first chapbook of poems, *The Colors of Water*, published by Finishing Line Press in 2007, and her second chapbook, *Moon Over Continent's Edge* (2009), have been nominated for a California Book Award. Her poems have also appeared in *PEARL, Fire, A New Song, Ancient Paths,* and *Knowing Stones: Poems of Exotic Places*. She earned her bachelor's degree in humanities and in history as well as a master's degree in history from Pepperdine University. An Educator Associate for the American Psychoanalytic Association, she lives in Newport Beach, California, with her husband.

KENDALL STEINLE grew up in Akron, Ohio. She attended Saint Xavier University in Chicago, along with a stint at the University of Glasgow, receiving her Bachelor's in English with minors in Writing and Middle Eastern Studies. Her first publication was in *Journal of Microliterature*. She is currently pursuing her master's degree in Writing and Publishing at DePaul University.

ADELLE STRIPE is a founding member of the Brutalist Poets and lives in Mytholmroyd, West Yorkshire. Her writing has appeared in *Mineshaft, Chiron Review,* and *PEARL.* She has released three poetry collections on Blackheath Books, and won Poetry Book of the Year

2009 at the 3:AM Magazine Awards. A new collection, *Dark Corners of the Land*, is due for publication at the end of 2012.

PAUL KAREEM TAYYAR, a three-time nominee for the Pushcart Prize, is the author of four collections of poetry: *Everyday Magic* (West-Coast Bias Press), *Scenes From A Good Life* (Tebot Bach), *Postmark Atlantis* (Level 4 Press), and *Follow the Sun: Poems, Stories, and Reflections* (Aortic Books). Paul's most recent book of prose is the novella *In the Footsteps of the Silver King* (Spout Hill Press). He is the Founding Director of World Parade Books, an independent press that has published works by Edward Field, Clifton Snider, and Donna Hilbert. He is one of the organizers of Beside the City of Angels: A Long Beach Poetry Festival.

KATI THOMSON is a writer residing in northern California. She describes herself as a one-time AP English geek and mother to two teenagers and a ten year old, who each represent a handful of other hungry noisy bodies. Her background is in nursing, and she worked in critical care, then pharmaceutical sales before deciding to follow more creative pursuits. Kati has written several short stories and poems, and is currently finishing her first novel, *Twine*. She is also involved in film, and served as executive producer of the documentary *Sunset Strip*, and is working on other projects currently in development. Her contribution to the *Silver Anthology* is the first chapter of a novella, *Yumyum*.

JERI THOMPSON, a former creative writing major who studied with Elliott Fried and Gerald Locklin at California State University, Long Beach, is currently a blogger (at Trikker Chicks…For Women Who Carve) and regular contributor to *TrikkeWorld* magazine. She can often be found walking around downtown Long Beach in bright blue Pumas or riding on a Trikke (with two Ks).

WINSTON TONG is a celebrated actor, playwright, visual artist, puppeteer, singer, and songwriter. He is best known for his vocal work in Tuxedomoon and for winning a 1978 Obie Award in puppetry for *Bound Feet*. He appeared in the 1981 documentary *Theater in Trance* by Rainer Werner Fassbinder, who shot the film at the Theaters of the World Festival in Cologne, Germany. Tong's career, including solo activity, was examined in detail in Isabelle Corbisier's Tuxedomoon biography *Music for Vagabonds—the Tuxedomoon Chronicles* (2008).

MARGARET TOWNER is a teacher of English learners and students at-risk in reading. She lived for many years in Latin America—Uruguay, Chile, El Salvador, and Mexico—and translates poetry from Spanish to English, writes children's music, and performs Latin American music. In 2005, she received the Jane Buel Bradley Chapbook Award, and her poetry will be featured in the *Cancer Poetry Project Anthology*, the Serving House Press, and the Center for Nondual Awareness.

MARY UMANS is a filmmaker and writer living in New York City. Her short film, *The Braddock Boys*, was featured in the 2012 Manhattan Film Festival.

DIRK VELVET is a Poet/Writer of Songs from Muskego, Wisconsin. His writing has been featured in *Beggars and Cheeseburgers, PEARL, Re)verb, Nerve Cowboy,* and *Milwaukee Renaissance.*

MELANIE VILLINES moved to Los Angeles from Chicago in 2007 and soon found a variety of writing assignments as an editor, ghostwriter, biographer, and screenwriter. Her published work includes the novel *Tales of the Sacred Heart* (Bogfire Press), the family memoir *Reason to Fight* (co-written with Hiram Johnson), a celebrity biography *Beyond Hollywood* (co-written with J. Herbert Klein), *Anna & Otto*, a novel for children (Inklings Press), and a variety of ghostwritten books and screenplays. In Chicago, she was active in the city's vibrant theater movement, studying with David Mamet and William H. Macy and co-founding the internationally acclaimed playwrights' development theater, Chicago Dramatists, where she workshopped fourteen of her plays. A theater company in Dallas has commissioned Melanie to write a stage play scheduled for a premiere in February 2013, and of the four screenplays she wrote in 2012, one has been optioned. Her contribution to the Silver Anthology ("Silver Bells, Silver Bells") is based on an incident in her life as a freelance writer.

FRED VOSS, a machinist for thirty-two years, has had three collections of poetry published by the U.K.'s Bloodaxe Books. He is regularly published in magazines such as *Poetry Review* (London), *Ambit* (London), *Rising* (London), *The Shop* (Ireland), *Atlanta Review,* and *PEARL*, and has twice been the subject of feature programs about his poetry on National BBC Radio 4. In 2008, he was featured at The Ledbury Poetry Festival, and in 2011 he and his wife, poet Joan Jobe Smith, were featured readers at the University of Pittsburgh and, in 2012 were featured at The Humber Mouth Literature Festival (Hull, England). His latest book, *Hammers and Hearts of the Gods* from Bloodaxe Books, was selected by U.K. newspaper *The Morning Star* as one of the Top Seven Books for 2009. In 2011, he was featured poet in a hardbound limited edition of *DWANG* (London, England), and in 2013 World Parade Books will publish his first novel, *Making America Strong*.

MARK WEBER corresponded with poet Jack Micheline in the late '80s when people used to type on rickety typewriters and fold the paper into stamped envelopes and give them to uniformed delivery people. Jack would draw funny pictures all over his "letter" (as people called them then). Mark left Southern California in 1986. He lived for a short spell in Redding, California, then shot across the land to Cleveland, Ohio, for three years, then back across to Salt Lake City, for two, and finally to Albuquerque in 1991. Mark is the publisher of Zerx Press classic 'zines. He is a gentleman house painter and radio disk jockey. See his website JAZZ FOR MOSTLY, markweber.free-jazz.net.

TIM WELLS likes reggae, beer, and pie 'n' mash. He lives in East London, United Kingdom.

STEVE WILLIAMS lives in Hollywood, California. He works as a carpenter throughout the West Coast and, on occasion, he writes.

PAMELA MILLER WOOD, a native Californian, has lived in the Los Angeles area most of her life. For over thirty years, she has enjoyed a successful career in the Southern California real estate industry, garnering many awards for outstanding achievement along the way, including Top Producer in Los Angeles County for ten consecutive years. *Charles Bukowski's Scarlet* is Pam's first full-length book—a memoir of her multi-year relationship with legendary author Charles Bukowski—a true tour de force.

www.ingramcontent.com/pod-product-compliance
Lightning Source LLC
Chambersburg PA
CBHW060257150626
46556CB00022B/2346